By The Same Author

HOME OF THE GODS

BEYOND THE TIME BARRIER

ANDREW TOMAS

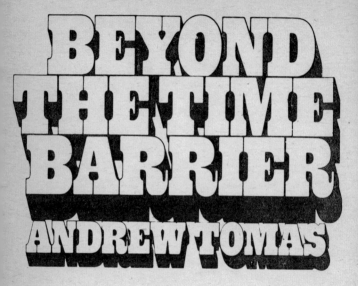

A BERKLEY MEDALLION BOOK
published by
BERKLEY PUBLISHING CORPORATION

*To my dear friend Dr. Miran Lindtner
of Sydney, Australia, whose active life
came to a tragic end at Frankfurt in 1969*

*BERKLEY MEDALLION BOOKS are published by
Berkley Publishing Corporation
200 Madison Avenue
New York, N.Y. 10016*

BERKLEY MEDALLION BOOK ® TM 757,375

Printed in the United States of America

Berkley Medallion Edition, FEBRUARY, 1976

CONTENTS

INTRODUCTION

This is an intellectual safari into that little explored desert of Time.

The nature of Time can become tangible only if the correlation between past, present and future is understood.

To know more about Time is "to be or not to be". To assess the present and perceive the future is like driving with headlights in the dark of night.

What is the Time Barrier? It is that instant known as NOW which separates the past from the future. If this razor-sharp barrier were broken, one could take a stroll into the future or journey into the past at will.

Our minds must be freed from the domination of the present. Only then will things be seen in their true light.

In this century of a chain reaction of scientific information when science fiction can hardly catch up with science, it is not futile to delve into the mystery of Time.

This problem concerns everyone because we all live in Time.

PART ONE

The problem of time

—

1. THE TRICKS OF CRONUS

THIS book is about Time and—

> *I'll tell thee everything I can*
> *There is little to relate.*
> *I saw an aged aged man,*
> *A-sitting on a gate.**

The aged man is, of course, Cronus or Saturn sitting on the gate to the future. Cronus devoured his children in order to remain immortal: Time consumes everything but remains indestructible.

Sinister as the old Saturn with the scythe and hour glass is, he lacks no sense of humour. This is fortunate because the riddles of Time are so grave. To cite Niels Bohr, these things "are so serious, you can only joke about them".

Because of the International Date Line and fast jet travel, passengers leaving Sydney for the United States at 17.00 hours land in San Francisco at 16.30 on the same day —in effect a half-hour before taking off!

In the First National City Bank of New York on the Champs Elysées in Paris, there are three wall clocks, marked New York, Paris and Tokyo.

A lady with a little girl stood at the counter one after-

*Lewis Carroll, *Through the Looking Glass.*

9

noon. The child was apparently baffled by the presence of three clocks showing different times—9, 2 and 11.

"Mamma, what's the time?"

"I think it's two o'clock, dear," replied the mother after finding the Paris clock.

"Why does it say 11 o'clock on that one?"

"That's Tokyo time," answered the lady.

"But is it 11 in the morning or at night?"

"Oh, how do I know? Can't you see I am busy with my cheques?"

As the child turned hopefully to me for the answer, I shrugged my shoulders in token of my pretended ignorance as I did not want to shake the lady's authority. However, parents who might find themselves in a similar embarrassing situation with their children, should bear in mind a useful piece of information: when it is 2 o'clock in the afternoon in Paris, it is 9 in the morning in New York and 11 the night before in Tokyo.

I left the bank and had a drink in a cafe nearby. It suddenly occurred to me that at that very moment a friend in Guatemala was having her breakfast and an acquaintance in Bombay was eating his curry-and-rice supper, while a colleague in Sydney was rolling his eyeballs in order not to miss anything in his first Freudian dream.

These examples illustrate one of the most complex concepts in physics—the relativity of simultaneity. What is *now* to one, is not necessarily *now* to another. Time is solidly welded to space and the point of reference.

An hour is also a measurement of space. It is an arc of 15 degrees in the apparent daily rotation of the celestial sphere. A year is nothing but one orbit of the Earth around the sun. A Martian year is almost twice as long because the orbit of Mars is larger. In everyday life Time is often identified with distance: "It is a five-minute walk to the station."

Einstein's Theory of Relativity shows that our attempt to separate the three dimensions of Space—breadth, depth and height—from Time is purely subjective. By referring our experiences to a clock or a calendar, we artificially create Time as an objective reality.

However, to define Time as an entirely subjective sensation is not altogether correct. Long before the advent of man, vast geological changes were taking place and strange, now-extinct animals roamed the planet but as a dimension Time already existed.

To show how relative Time is, let us analyse the flight of an astronaut around the earth. Cape Kennedy rotates around the planetary axis once in twenty-four hours. But the U.S. astronaut orbits the planet in some 90 minutes, so he sees sixteen "days" while we see only one. The length of the day is thus decided by the speed of rotation around the axis. If the astronaut is paid wages by the day, he should get sixteen times more than the technician on the ground, provided NASA accepts his calendar.

In *The Conquest of Time* H. G. Wells gives a good example of the relative significance of Time. He imagines himself standing on the North Pole and looking at the sun. It is 12 o'clock on Sunday. As he rotates with the Earth on top of the planet, it remains 12 o'clock on Sunday until he makes a complete revolution when it becomes 12 o'clock on Monday. What happens if one begins to turn oneself faster than the Earth? One gets to the starting-point sooner than the Earth.

History knows of a few oddities for which the god Cronus is certainly responsible. When the survivors of the Magellan expedition reached Spain aboard the *Victoria* under the command of Captain Elcano on September 7, 1522, they discovered, to their amazement, that in spite of an accurately kept log-book, a day had been lost during their westward voyage around the globe. As the seamen

11

had not celebrated holy days on the right days, the Church asked them to do penance. We know now that the log-book of Magellan was correct and the penance should be credited to the souls of the sailors. In circumnavigating the Earth the explorers lost a day because there was no International Date Line in those times.

So that a similar oddity should not happen again, ocean liners travelling from San Francisco to Tokyo have two Sundays or Wednesdays in one week.

The story of Magellan is the tale of one lost day, and not so bad as the case of eleven days which were torn off the calendars in 1732. England adopted the Gregorian calendar in that year and dropped eleven days. A riot was immediately staged by workers who demanded wages for the missing days.

In ancient times it was the business of priests, poets and philosophers to meditate upon Time and in the words of Shakespeare—

> To see the minutes how they run,
> How many makes the hour full complete;
> How many hours bring about the day;
> How many days will finish up the year;
> How many years a mortal man may live.*

That was an epoch when a minute was a minute and an hour an hour. In the last seven decades science has discovered that the world does not consist of points but of events. Nothing can exist in space unless it also exists in Time. Likewise nothing can have being in Time unless it has a place in space.

Unexplored regions have opened before our mental gaze. In the newly discovered curvature of space, straight lines vanished from the universe. Time had become dependent on the observer at a certain point in space. This was not

*Henry VI, III, 2, Scene 5.

12

only a revolution in science but an explosion of the myth that Time was something abstract—beyond the universe.

2. GHOST STARS

ONE NIGHT in 1972 a Greenwich astronomer studied the star Polaris. It was about 4 o'clock in the morning and he decided to telephone his colleague at Mount Palomar Observatory to check his observations. It was 8 o'clock at night in California and his American confrère agreed to have a look at the star. Soon they were watching their star at the "same time" although to one it was the end of the night and to the other—the beginning. What is more, the astronomers were studying the Polaris as it was in 1922 because the light from the star takes fifty years to reach the Earth.

It is an awe-inspiring sight to watch the stars on a clear night. Everyone has seen the three stars of the belt of Orion as well as Betelgeuse and Rigel. However, not everyone knows that the light from Betelgeuse reaches the Earth in 275 years. In other words, it is seen today as *it was* when Peter the Great visited Holland. Rigel is farther away at a distance of 540 light years. We observe the star tonight not as it really is at this moment, but as it was in the days when Jeanne d'Arc led the army of France.

The arch of the Milky Way is made up of millions of stars which are thousands of light years away. From the Southern hemisphere one can see the Magellanic Clouds, vast star-clouds situated near our Milky Way galaxy at a distance of 150,000 light years from our planet. This means that they appear tonight as they were at a time when the primitive man of the Paleolithic era first discovered fire.

The Galaxy 3C-295 in Boötes is 5,000 million light years from the solar system. The astronomer studies merely a past image of this galaxy from a time when the Earth was not in existence. He may be watching *nothing* from *nowhere* if the galaxy had exploded in the meantime.

Even the sun in the sky is not perceived by us at this instant—what we see and feel now are the rays of the sun which left it eight minutes ago. Sparkling Venus is a picture of the planet as it was two minutes ago.

What we behold in space is a vision of innumerable pasts. The stars in the heavens are nothing but a multitude of stellar portraits taken a few years or a few thousand years ago. There is not a single object in space that can be seen at this moment. Fast as the speed of light is—300,000 kilometres per second, it still takes time for it to reach our world.

We never see the stars as they are now, because our NOW is not identical with their present. The stars in the sky are nothing but *ghost stars*. The stars shifted in the Milky Way galaxy years ago, so they are not where they seem to be now.

3.   THE OLD UNIVERSE IN A NEW FRAME

In the pre-Einsteinian epoch a straight line was the shortest distance between two points. A metre was a metre everywhere and under all circumstances. *Tick-Tock* Time was something concrete that could be measured by a clock as exactly as a path with a metre tape.

In Newton's definition "absolute, true and mathematical time passes continually, and by virtue of its nature flows uniformly and without regard to any external object what-soever'. He did not say where this 'stream of Time' was coming from, nor where it was going.

Then came Albert Einstein and the Euclidean world collapsed like a card castle. On the blackboard he chalked out new formulas involving mass, energy, light velocity and time. The equations produced revolutionary results. The old metre with its hundred centimetres suddenly ceased to be dependable. If the scale flew in a photon spaceship at a speed approaching that of light, it would shrink to about half its length!

Straight lines began to develop a tendency to curl like ladies' hair in a beauty salon. The whole universe was soon found to exist in curved space.

All measurements of Time came to be regarded as measurements of space. Time was discovered to be a dimension of space. The German physicist Minkowski formulated this thought in his famous words: "Henceforth Space by itself and Time by itself shall sink to mere shadows and only a union of the two shall preserve reality."

Objects must be regarded as existing in four dimensions, three of these being the ordinary ones of length, breadth and thickness, and the fourth—Time. The space continuum cannot begin to exist until the Time dimension is supplied, nor can Time have being apart from Space.

It is necessary to note here that the Time co-ordinate is physically different from the Space co-ordinates, although they cannot exist without each other. According to Einstein, the difference is only qualitative.

Realising the impact that all these discoveries in physics were making on the minds of his contemporaries, Einstein said: "The non-mathematician is seized by a strange horror if he hears of four-dimensional objects, just as if it were some concept of the occult. Moreover, he cannot see that it is nothing more than an artificial concept when we say that the world in which we live is a four-dimensional Space-Time continuum."

The River of Time which washed away races, civilisations and planets in our concept, was no longer flowing. The realisation came that people and objects move in Space-Time.

Time and Space cannot be destroyed because they are not things but dimensions. Whole universes of stars can decay and become cosmic dust. Space will still be there, waiting to give birth to other worlds.

The Time co-ordinate is a womb of cosmic events as something is always happening in the infinite universe.

Time is not a straight line with a red dot jumping on it called NOW. It is the spiral of eternal recurrence.

The Time rate seems immutable yet this is but an illusion. Time is measured by periodic motion. If this rhythm is slowed down, Time also will slow down.

From Einstein's Theory of Relativity many conclusions can be drawn. All time processes will be slower on a large mass than on a small one. They are slow in the infinitely great such as a galaxy, and rapid in the world of the atom.

Time processes are relative and dependent on the size of objects. Our Milky Way galaxy is more than 10 milliard years old. On the other hand, mesons and hyperons live but a fraction of a second.

From the relativist view every reference system has its own, special time. When the old universe was put into this new frame, it became apparent that reality in another point of Space-Time might be as valid as that which we perceive HERE—NOW.

To illustrate the relative character of the present let us imagine that in 1700 (by terrestrial chronology) an intelligent radio message was transmitted from a planet rotating around Betelgeuse in Orion. This message will be received by Jodrell Bank radio telescope in 1975, because the Earth is 275 light years distant from the star*. However, the inhabitants of a planet in the system of Aldebaran in Taurus would have already received it in 1925 because they are 50 light years closer to Betelgeuse. It can be seen from this hypothetical case that one and the same event does not take place at the same time in three different systems. This event—the transmission of a radio message and its reception by two solar systems involves three dates—1700, 1925 and 1975.

The HERE—NOW of each observer is an arbitrary point in Space-Time and has no absolute significance.

When Professor Franck was being installed in the faculty of physics at the University of Prague, the dean gravely warned him: "We ask you to behave yourself normally."

"What? Is this so rare among the physicists?" asked the new professor.

"You do not mean to say that your predecessor was normal?" responded the dean. The predecessor's name was Albert Einstein.

4. TRAVEL FAST, AGE SLOWLY

IT WAS THE ancient Greeks who first tried to solve the problems of Time, Space and Motion but only in the twentieth century did we finally get the right answers.

An increase in velocity of a moving body reduces the time needed to cover a certain distance. On the other hand, a decrease in speed means an increase in time required to traverse an extension of space.

The distance between Paris and Tours is approximately 230 kilometres, and a car travelling from Paris at the speed of about 115 kilometres per hour will reach Tours in two

*Radio waves travel at the same speed as light.

hours. However, should the car race at 230 kilometres per hour, it would arrive one hour earlier. The Time required for reaching the destination has shrunk one-half because of an increase in velocity.

One of the most curious conclusions scientists make from relativist equations, concerns time dilation. Time slows down on a body flying at an extremely high velocity.

From Lorenz contraction and Einstein time-dilation formulae it appears that interstellar tourists flying at a speed close to that of light will assume strange shapes. A pretty girl will be squashed like an accordion or become as flat as a flounder, and think nothing of it. What is more, the captain of a spaceship would maintain that the young lady is still beautiful. Time will crawl so slowly that it will be decades from lunch to dinner but no one will protest against this outrage. In this weird situation the girl will have to regard her trip amongst the stars as a rejuvenation operation because the rocket ship will hurl her into a distant century.

In this Space Age it is quite proper to speak of spaceships. To cover interstellar space man will require ships that fly at a speed approaching that of light, or just below 300,000 kilometres per second. Although blueprints of photon and anti-matter cosmic rockets exist, it will take many decades for astronautical engineers to solve construction problems connected with these spacecraft.

Nonetheless, we can picture a hypothetical voyage of such a rocket in cosmic space. Because of an incredible acceleration all time processes in the spaceship will be retarded.

The atoms of the rocket, the cells of the astronauts' bodies, the air, water and food supplies in the spaceship will slow down at a uniform rate. The respiration, heartbeat, digestion, nervous and mental processes of the astronauts will be slowed, too. This retardation would not be noticed by the occupants of the ship because the chronometer would slow correspondingly.

Their log-book would have a new page and date every twenty-four hours. Meals would be eaten at the usual times and the astronauts would sleep after work. Nothing would indicate that in relation to the Earth which they had left, their time assumed a different pace.

Let us suppose that a space probe of the Pleiades will be launched by the International Space Administration in 2050. The nearest Pleiades are roughly at distance of eleven light years from our planet.

The spaceship *Terra 328* after reaching destination, swerves without losing acceleration and returns to the Earth. According to the captain's log-book the voyage took twenty-two years and the date is 2072.

However, when they land, the captain is in far worse trouble than Magellan's seamen with their calendar difference of one day.

First of all, the base cannot be located. Except for most of the geographical features, the Earth seems to be a different planet. Some cities cannot be found on the map, others have sprung up. Their own countrymen speak a different dialect. But a greater shock is in store for the crew. The Earth calendar shows the year 3050! The captain was thirty-three when he left and is now fifty-five years old. Yet 1,000 years have elapsed according to the Earth's calendars. And so space travel turned into Time travel for they whizzed 978 years into the future.

More pathetic incidents can be imagined in future astronavigation. A 25-year-old astronaut has a lovely wife of the same age. He embarks on a distant voyage to the star Vega. After a non-stop flight, which occupies 14 years, he is about to celebrate his 39th birthday. When he lands on the Earth, an old lady of 90 is brought to the spacedrome in a wheelchair to meet him. That is his wife! Due to time dilation on the spaceship he travelled for only 14 years but his wife aged 65 years on the Earth*.

The time lapse was short for the astronaut and long for the Earth-dweller.

It is possible that certain historical records speak of this time dilation. In the *Vision of Isaiah*† the prophet is taken to heaven by an angel. When he returns to Earth after a stay amidst the stars for two weeks, Isaiah is shocked to find out that 32 years have passed since his departure. Can it be assumed that the angel was a being from a planet with photon-ray spaceships?

In the case of two spaceships flashing past each other at speeds close to that of light, will Time shrink to nothing?

> *There was a young lady named Bright*
> *Whose speed was much faster than light,*
> *She set out one day,*
> *In a relative way,*
> *To return on the previous night!*

It is apparent that in fast cosmic cruises voyagers will preserve their youth. However, the slogan *Travel Fast— Age Slowly* applies only to interstellar travel.

Travelling at excessive speeds on highways can age one prematurely in a sudden car accident.

5. CLOCKS AND THE SOUL

MOST PROBLEMS OF contemporary physics could be resolved if the essence of Time was understood. Scientists admit that in physics Time is the most elusive and frus-

---

*These examples are based on different velocities of interstellar spaceships, producing different time shrinkages.

†R. H. Charles, *Epigraphia and Pseudoepigraphia of the Old Testament*, London, 1910.

trating principle. However, this mystery should be taken as a challenge and an invitation to explore further.

"The most beautiful and most profound emotion we can experience is the sensation of the mystical. It is the sower of all true science. He to whom this emotion is a stranger, who can no longer wonder and stand rapt in awe, is as good as dead," said Einstein.

From this point of view no effort should be spared in trying to find definitions of something that can probably be described only in terms of abstract ideas, mathematics or by means of allegories.

It was the ancient Greek philosopher Heraclitus who thus spoke of Time: "You cannot step into the same river twice, for other waters are ever flowing on."

Time and consciousness are closely linked. In the *psyche* Time may be the principal dimension. In the physical world we move in space by means of Time—it takes us a given length of time to perform certain actions, such as walking. In the mental world we move in Time by reminiscing past events, while occupying space—sitting in an armchair, for example.

Our time sense does not always give us the correct estimation of duration. One hour may seem long but another short. It is emotional reaction that colours the impressions.

If one hears a boring lecture or waits for a train at the station "time drags on". If a person attends a party and has "a good time", time flies.

Long before the birth of the Theory of Relativity, Shakespeare wrote: "Time travels in divers paces with divers persons."

If a great number of events take place in a limited period of time in a new environment, the period seems to be much longer than it really is. Mr. Brown, a London businessman, went through the same office routine on Wednesday,

Thursday and Friday. He arrived at 9.30 in the morning and left at 6 p.m. Then he had his dinner and watched television. On Friday night he boarded a plane for Paris and had a stroll along the Champs Elysées. On Saturday morning he visited the Louvre, saw Paris from the Eiffel Tower, and enjoyed his lunch in a topnotch restaurant. Then he flew to Nice, basked in the sun on the Côte d'Azur, had a few drinks, following which he had supper and slept in the hotel. On Sunday he was in Venice with its canals and gondolas. On Monday morning he took a plane for Zurich—where he saw the clear blue sky and blinding snow of the Alps. Late on Monday night he was back in London where it was drizzling. On Tuesday morning Mr. Brown was not himself. It seemed to him that he had been away for at least a week or ten days. Saturday, Sunday, and Monday were much longer to him than Wednesday, Thursday and Friday.

A rapid flow of Time in a dream is another strange psychological phenomenon. During the French Revolution the Marquis de Lavalette experienced a dream while he was in prison and the clock was striking twelve. Events of five hours were seen by him in less than a minute: "I was in the Rue Saint Honoré. It was dark and streets deserted, but soon a diffused dull murmur was heard. Suddenly a troop of horsemen appeared at the end of the street— terrible beings, bearing torches. For five hours they passed me by, riding at full gallop. After them came a vast number of gun carriages loaded with dead bodies."

Professor Vasilieff refers to the case of a famous playwright who came to see the performance of his stage play but went to sleep in his seat. In the dream he saw his play from beginning to end and watched the reaction of the audience. At last the curtain went down to thunderous applause and the playwright woke up in surprise to hear but the first sentences of the dialogue in Act One. The duration of the performance of the whole piece on the stage in his dream had thus taken only a few seconds*.

The acceleration of events in dreams is quite common. There is another psychological phenomenon in which memories of a whole life flash in seconds before one's mind. Drowning or a mortal danger brings on this state in which one's life unfolds like a motion picture in a few seconds.

An acquaintance of the author in Moscow, an engineer, was knocked down and injured in the Metro several years ago. In the course of seconds his long life arose before his mental vision, complete in every detail. He was not sure whether he moved through the episodes of his life at a fabulous speed, or if the chain of happenings from infancy to the day of his accident appeared all together, as in a vast painting.

Skydiver Bob Hall, who survived a jump when his parachute failed to open, thus relates his experience: "I screamed. I knew I was dead. That my life was ended. All my past life flashed before my eyes, it really did."†

Drugs such as mescalin, hashish or opium can cause visions in which the events of decades are compressed into a few brief hours.

Many years ago the author had a Chinese cook in Shanghai who was an opium addict. One night he was the Emperor of China in the Peking Palace surrounded by beautiful wives and concubines. On another occasion he was a pirate in the China sea. Then came the exciting night when he was a Taoist alchemist making gold by ingots. The amazing thing about these psychological films was their acceleration—long lives being squeezed into a few short hours.

*L. L. Vasilieff, *Mysterious Phenomena of Human Consciousness*, Moscow, 1964 (Russian).
†*Time*, Dec. 4, 1972.

One morning the cook was sad and I asked him why he was so depressed. "Last night I was a cook," he said. I told him that it was no use smoking opium any more—it was merely a waste of money and a risk to his health. "But how do I know that I am not dreaming now that I am only a cook?' he asked. That reminded me of the tale of *Through the Looking Glass* in which Alice says: "So I wasn't dreaming after all—unless, unless we're all part of the same dream."

The French speleologist Michel Siffre spent sixty days in caverns in 1962. In this experiment he was deprived of methods to measure time and had to rely on his biological clock. When he emerged out of the dark underworld, Siffre thought he had spent only thirty-three days in the caves.

On January 15, 1969, two French spelunkers surfaced at the end of a five-month cave-living experiment organised by Michel Siffre. Jacques Chabert and Phillipe Englander entered the caves in the south of France in the middle of August, 1968. When they emerged from their solitary confinement in two separate caves, both thought it was November 15, 1968, instead of January 15, 1969. With no watches, depending on their biological time-sense alone, they were two months behind in their estimation of Time.

Businessmen making frequent jet flights across continents complain of the difficulties they have in adjusting to time changes. They find it hard to adopt new eating and sleeping hours in places with different time. Evidently their biological clock protests against the sudden change of geographical time.

Gautama the Buddha was aware of the subjective character of Time when he asked a Brahmin these questions two and a half thousand years ago:

"Where is your self? Your self to which you cleave is a constant change. Years ago you were a baby. Then you were a boy, then a youth and now you are a man. Is there any identity of the baby and the man? Which is your self —that of yesterday, that of today, or that of tomorrow for the preservation of which you are so longing?"

"You have confused me," responded Kutadanta, the Brahmin.

The duration of Time is assessed by man in different ways. As the Buddha said: "Long is the night to him who cannot sleep. Long is a mile to the weary."

The central thought in understanding Time is the realisation that Time does not flow. It is matter and consciousness that move through Space-Time. Time is an endless road with constantly changing landscapes, some of which we create ourselves before we arrive at a given point in the future.

6. NIRVANA AND THE ATOM

TWENTY-FIVE CENTURIES ago a man sat under a wild-fig tree in Gaya in the valley of the Ganga and said: "Not until I gain wisdom will I move from this tree." For forty-nine days he remained under the shadow of the tree. In his meditations he solved the mystery of Good and Evil, Life and Time. Like branches of that wild-fig tree his thoughts grew until they embraced the cosmos. Thus he became the enlightened one, or the Buddha.

Then he said: "I believe that the world is going to exist forever and forever. It will never come to an end. And anything that has no end, has no beginning. The world was not created by anyone. The world always was."

If the universe had not existed eternally, a difficult question arises—what was before it? St. Augustine reflected upon the problem and asked—what did God do before

Creation? Reasonable theological and philosophical answers have been given. But the most amusing is the one which says that God was building an inferno for people who ask silly questions.

The Big Bang Theory or the origin of the universe from a single atom suggests a beginning in Time. The Steady State Theory opposes it and offers a picture of eternal creation and destruction. The two theories can be reconciled by a concept of a pulsating metagalaxy, without a beginning or end.

Whether or not there is anyone on Earth to wind a clock in a milliard years from now, Time as a dimension will not vanish. When our planet is reduced to cosmic dust, the imprint of life in ancient Egypt, on the tropic islands of Oceania, in the snows of the Himalayas, will remain on the highway of Time.

The amount of rainfall in the year 1750 can be measured by tree rings. By a carbon-14 test it is possible to determine the age of a pharaoh's sarcophagus. From ancient clays it is ascertained which way the compass needle pointed fifteen thousand years ago. By a time-thermometer the scientists are able to find out the life span of a mollusc that lived one hundred and fifty million years ago, and the temperature of sea water at that time.

"Everything exists, and not one sigh, nor smile, no tear, one hair, nor particle of dust, not one can pass away," wrote William Blake.

Nature may be recording everything that happens. This is quite possible in Teilhard de Chardin's philosophy of the conscious atom. This concept is not new—in India the essence of matter is called Akasa or Prakriti.

Ever since Francis Bacon, the learned of Europe have been discarding doubtful metaphysics in favour of physics. An age of Science and Technology was created to enjoy and to fear. Then unexpectedly in the twentieth century a tendency to slide back into metaphysics has appeared. The Absolute Time of Newton gave way to the Relativist Time of Einstein. The old-fashioned spherical atom deemed to be as solid as a grain of sand, turned into a system of superimposed waves and charges. And, horror of horrors, matter was discovered to be empty space with specks of electricity—the electrons. And if this were not enough, the wall between the animate and the inanimate began to crumble. "Matter has been dematerialised," declared Professor N. R. Hanson.

7. TWO WORLDS IN ONE

THE DISCOVERY OF antiparticles is one of the most revolutionary developments of nuclear physics. Besides the atom with a positive proton and negatively-charged electron, science knows of the antiproton and the positron. The exploration of the micro-world has disclosed the presence of antimatter in the universe. Scientists speak of antistars and antigalaxies. They say that the antiworld behaves exactly as if it were a reflection of our world.

Somewhere in space there may be an antiplanet with antisnow caps on its antipoles. It may be inhabited by our cosmic antipodes. Unfortunately, we shall never meet them because if our spaceship tried to land on an antiplanet, a tremendous explosion would take place as matter and antimatter annihilated each other.

Whether antimatter is scattered throughout the visible universe or spread in patches outside of our galaxy, is still an open question.

In view of the fact that the antiworld and our world can not come into contact, we are faced with the astonishing concept of two worlds living side by side.

In physics the positron is defined as an electron moving backwards in Time*. The direction of Time in the anti-world is from the future to the past.

E. I. Parnov writes in *Where Infinities Meet*: "In principle, man could have possessed the freedom to sail on the waves of Time which atomic particles have. But it so happened that, for some reason, man is made of particles and not of antiparticles, and particles move in the direction of the future."

According to Professor Hans Reichenbach, the imaginary inhabitants of some antigalaxy would regard their Time as forward and ours as backward. This Time reversal in the antiworld is one of its strangest features.

A British physicist F. Russell Stannard in speaking of the hypothetical dwellers of that other world, which he calls *Faustian*, claims that living organisms would grow young and though entropy† would be decreasing in a universe where Time goes backward, the intelligent beings of that world would not notice anything peculiar in their environment. In the antiworld an aged lady would be getting younger and younger without being aware of her rejuvenation! It is a pity that this secret of youth cannot be brought to Earth for use by those who have reached the autumn of their lives.

An argument between worlds may arise. The antipeople would be convinced it is they who age, and we who grow younger. It is not easy to picture a world gliding from the future into the past.

In a mix-up like this how can we determine which is past and which is future? Sir Arthur Eddington has given a good definition of the *Arrow of Time*:

*Dr. Richard Feinman received a Nobel Prize in 1965 for this discovery.

†The increasing heat dissipation in the universe towards a uniform temperature.

"If as we follow the arrow we find more and more of the random element in the state of the world, then the arrow is pointing towards the future. If the random element decreases, the arrow points towards the past. That is the only distinction known to physics.*"

Time direction is relative, as relative as the concept of UP or DOWN. It would be meaningless to say that the entire universe turned upside down, or suddenly reversed its Time direction. There is no absolute UP or DOWN or FORWARD or BACKWARD in the cosmos.

Time reversal in the antiworld is a discovery which opens new perspectives. "Can we, like the electrons, reverse our travel in Time?" asks the Soviet scientist E. I. Parnov. "The answer is not devoid of humour. Had a man decided to do so, he would have already known about it ... somewhere in the future. We know what is taking place around us at a given moment. The world axis which is to be reversed, will nevertheless pass through the present—that is through this very moment. All this certainly sounds fantastic but only because we deal with people, and not with elementary particles."

Can Time go backward? This problem was studied by the great Plato. Twenty-four centuries ago he wrote in *The Statesman* about an oscillating universe, periodically reversing its Time arrow. At the end of each cycle Time stops and then everything moves backward. In this reversal of Time old men become young, strong and handsome until they find themselves crying in the cradle and then disappearing in the mother's womb—instead of the grave.

The fanciful notion of Plato echoes now in the field of nuclear physics. Tachyons or atomic particles travelling faster than light, move backwards in Time—says Dr. Gerald Feinberg of Columbia University.

*Space, Time and Gravitation, Cambridge, 1920.

Although according to the Theory of Relativity no atomic particle can be accelerated to a velocity beyond that of light, in theory there can exist particles which have had the initial speed faster than light. These particles can never slow down. Tachyons would possess "negative energy", "imaginary mass" and "backward time". A search for these atomic particles is now under way.

It is amazing to find the idea of Reverse Time in the writings of Swedenborg who claimed that "in Heaven the angels are advancing continually to the springtime of their youth so that the oldest angel appears to be the youngest." Is this Heaven then an antiworld or a parallel universe?

Einstein has demonstrated that there are no straight lines in space. If the Time co-ordinate is also curved, many things concerning the arrow of Time become clear. Let us draw a circumference and divide it in half horizontally. Imagine a point moving from left to right on the upward arc to symbolise the forward Time of our world. Let the downward arc be the backward Time of the antiworld with a dot moving from right to left. Although the Time directions are opposite, forward Time can become backward Time once the demarcation line between worlds is passed. It is another question whether an intercourse between the two worlds with different polarities is possible at all. If there is a curvature of Time, one can develop such science-fiction notions as Hyper-Time of Isaac Asimov, the possibility of touching the past or future by bending Time. It is an old idea that Time is bent. In ancient symbology Time is portrayed as a serpent swallowing its own tail.

Concurrent with the mental image of the antiworld is the concept of a parallel universe. Neutrinos, those spinning sub-atomic particles with neither charge nor mass, shoot through our solid planet as if it were made of nothing. Were the Earth a million times bigger, neutrinos would still be able to penetrate it at the velocity of light.

The neutrino world can actually co-exist with our own.

The distinguished Oxford physicist D. H. Wilkinson has a perfect right to theorise that "perhaps there do exist universes interpenetrating with ours; perhaps of a high complexity; perhaps containing their own forms of awareness; constructed out of other particles and other interactions than those which we now know, but awaiting discovery through some common but elusive interaction that we have yet to spot".*

These novel ideas in physics can throw light on the mystery of Time and are presented for that reason. A parallel universe could have its own special Time which may not necessarily correspond with ours. Its temporal range may be wider and an ascent to that level may extend the frontiers of Time.

8. THE LONGEST MOTION PICTURE EVER SHOWN

"DAYS AND NIGHTS pass, and ages bloom and fade like flowers," wrote Tagore reflecting upon Time.

Whence have we come? Where are we at present? Whither are we going in the March of Time? These questions are neither abstract nor idle—they concern our lives.

Modern physics recognises no stream of Time. Time as an integral dimension of Space, can no more flow than breadth, length or thickness.

Sir Arthur Eddington has thus formulated the movement of things and beings in Space-Time: "This division into past and future is closely associated with our ideas of causation and freewill. In a perfectly determinate scheme, the past and future may be regarded as lying

*J. B. Priestley, *Man and Time*, New York, 1964.

mapped out—as much available to present exploration as the distant parts of space. Events do not happen, they are just there, and we come across them."*

Not all scientists agree with a determinism of this sort because of the unpredictable elements in the future.

The present is a tiny differential between two infinite extensions—the past and the future. Mathematically, this differential or NOW is equal to zero. How long does NOW last? Is it a microsecond or less? One can divide NOW into smaller fractions of the microsecond without ever catching the present instant.

The past is something that already does not exist. The future does not yet exist. The present is here. The only instant that seems real is the intangible moment of transition of the future into the present, and of the present into the past. However, how can anything be real if it serves as a link between two unrealities? We have either to say that the present also does not exist, which is an absurdity, or to assume that both the past and the future have realities of their own. Evidently, our mind is unable to grasp Time in its wider perspective, as a continuous past-present-future extension.

The gallery of Time shows a succession of NOWS. The only way to distinguish them is by realising that some are AFTER or BEFORE others. Events which are after the present are understood as future. Happenings which lie before the present are considered past. Without an arbitrary point TODAY or NOW from which events are viewed, it would be impossible to know which is past or future.

Though the future is not crystallised, some things are fixed—the length of life of an animal, for example. Time does not extend from the present into a non-being because something always happens in the infinite universe. This is

*A. Eddington, *Space, Time and Gravitation*, Cambridge, 1920.

a more complete picture of Time, or else the Time dimension would look like a cinema reel with half of it utterly missing. That film of future Time may be partially blank or undeveloped, but it is before us.

Lost in the vast expanse of the Atlantic at St. Helena, Napoleon once mused: "If I can span the space from St. Helena, why not that of the centuries? Why should I not see the future like the past?"

From a philosophic and scientific viewpoint, determinism cannot provide the right answers to the problem of Time. Neither can the philosophy of probability which regards the world as an eternal roulette. Possibly, the riddle of the future can be solved by reconciling the two opposite schools.

Present, past and future might be defined in the following way: that which was actualised is the past, that which is possible is the future, and the process of actualisation is the present.

It is in the future that the possibilities of today are materialised. The future is a field of crystallisation of these probabilities and has a reality of its own. It cannot be a vacuum because it issues from the present which is not empty. The division of Time into the three sections is merely qualitative.

It is erroneous to regard the past as a phantom. Activity in the physical and mental worlds is recorded every second. The bark rings of a tree indicate its age. Rocks disclose their age by magnetism. Archaeological remains leave a record of past history. Whether or not we are aware of it, the past has a real existence. It is not a waste-paper basket for used events. The future is not the contents of Fortune's horn emptied at random.

Life is an infinite series of NOWS like a motion picture with a million film frames. This cinema picture seems continuous because the NOWS never stop.

It is apparent that the present is relative. The present of the people living at the time of Napoleon Bonaparte was different from ours. To that epoch we were a generation of the future. Destiny is always young and history is being written today. What is the future to us, will be the present to our descendants.

The sages of India meditated upon the nature of Time and arrived at thoroughly scientific conclusions. The three-faced Trimurti was invented by them to symbolise Three-Faced-Time. Brahma created the visible world in the past, Vishnu preserves it in the present, and Shiva will destroy creation in the future to build new worlds out of the debris of the old. Death appears at the feast of life but life is always born at the funeral of worlds.

The difficulty in understanding the substance of Time lies in our inability to view it objectively for in the words of Niels Bohr "we are both spectators and actors in the great drama of existence."

In the dance, tragedy, pantomime and comedy which we call life, there is an element of unreality. The procession of Time is real with all its joys and sorrows if one takes a part in it. But if it were possible to look at history from the outside, the sense of its dramatic actuality might be lost.

Shakespeare had deep insight into the mystery of Time when he wrote:

> *All the world's a stage*
> *And all the men and women merely players:*
> *They have their exits and their entrances . . .* *

Do we repeat the words of a fixed script on the stage of life, or do we improvise our acts? Our past follows us like a black shadow. What we are today is the result of our desires, thoughts and actions of yesterday. In some ways we seem to have freedom of choice, in others—none. If

As You Like It, II, 7.

a country is hit by a war, one is more likely to suffer than escape its ravages. If a man is old and in poor health, he will not live another twenty-five years. A man with little training or education is not likely to succeed in life. Often a man's fate is on his face. There is one thing of which we may be certain—past causes invisibly project effects into the future.

Is history a long motion picture film that stretches from the dawn of civilisation to distant epochs? Does this film exist in a dimension that in this world we are not able to perceive?

If we were creatures of two dimensions on a flat surface and a sphere was going through it, we would first see a dot becoming a circle and then the circle becoming a dot again. The two-dimensional beings of the Flatland would not be in a position to understand the appearance and disappearance of the circle. In like manner a phenomenon from a higher dimension may pose a riddle in our Space-Time world.

Life can be compared to a concerto based on time and rhythm. The conductor remembers the whole musical composition and times its performance with his baton. A future musical note becomes a sound in the present instant. The conductor has to be one step ahead to anticipate the next notes. In the flow of music he knows the future. The conductor has freewill to improvise a little without upsetting the orchestra.

Perhaps a similar thing is taking place in the world. Life is a cosmic composition but we improvise to some extent.

Time is usually interpreted by us as long or short. But it can also be broad or narrow. The number of probabilities and the scope of action determine this breadth.

In the past lies not only that which actually took place but also that which could have been. Everyone has a number of different versions of his life.

In the future rests not only that which will be but also that which may be. The future has breadth as an arena of possibilities.

Professor Reichenbach asks the burning question: "What is it, this future? Does it keep events in stock, so to speak, or distribute them according to a plan? Or do events grow from chance?"*

Future events pre-exist as projects of realisable possibilities. These projects on the temporal axis can sometimes be predicted. Autumn is expected after summer. Halley's Comet will appear about 1986. A doctor can tell when a patient afflicted by a fatal disease will die.

Potentially, a human being has a number of lives which may be lived. They are like cinema reels and one has to decide which is to be projected on the screen. But by force of circumstance, it is often impossible to select the desired version of one's life story. Then nothing is left to do but to drift on the ocean of life, borne by the winds of destiny or those social, economic and psychological factors which have one in their grip. The life of an individual is inseparable from the society of which he is a particle. However, as a spiritual being, man is free and his frontiers stretch to infinity.

Although death hurls a person into Eternity he still belongs to Time because Eternity is All-Time. There are two interpretations of Eternity. It is nothing else but an infinite extension of Time, says one. Anderson M. Scruggs has put this idea into poetry:

> *Eternity is here—not far away,*
> *In some dim region none has ever known;*
> *It is this hour, this minute, this day . . .*

The other concept identifies Eternity with a timeless state from which events can be seen all at once—past,

*H. Reichenbach, *The Direction of Time*, University of California, 1956.

present and future. Thomas Vaughan wrote a verse about this in the 16th century:

> *I saw Eternity the other night*
> *Like a great Ring of pure and endless light,*
> *All calm, as it was bright,*
> *And round beneath it, Time in hours, days, years,*
> *Driven by the spheres*
> *Like a vast shadow moved.*

To solve the enigma of Time it is necessary to analyse opposing views.

9. SMASHING THE NOW

TIME CONSTANTLY sways us. The dramatic reality of a motion picture is not questioned during its performance. Voices of singers who died long ago such as Caruso or Chaliapin can still be heard on discs.

The qualitative sections of Time—past, present and future—are continually replacing each other. What is NOW at present will be past in an instant, and what is future at this moment, will eventually become the present. Time is an infinite number of NOWS welded into a Time curve.

To understand Time we must have a correct appreciation of the relation between the past, present and future.

Henri Bergson defined duration as the continuous progress of the past which gnaws into the future. The American philosopher Will Durant wrote that as the motion picture camera takes numerous static photographs, so our intellect has a series of states. Without continuity these states would be as meaningless as a single frame in a long film.

Hindu sages have come to profound conclusions about

Time: "The present is the child of the past; the future, begotten of the present, and yet, o present moment! knowest thou not that thou hast no parent nor canst thou have a child; that thou art ever begetting but thyself? before thou hast even begun to say 'I am the progeny of the departed moment, the child of the past', thou hast become that past itself, before thou utterest the very last syllable, behold! thou art no more the present but verily that future."

Whether or not Time is an illusion, or Maya, hinges on the concrete reality of the present. If NOW is real then yesterday and tomorrow live today. NOW is a focus through which the pent-up energies of the past are refracted into probable actions in the future.

Time is an endless chain of events in which every link has a tangible reality. The links behind are as real as the ones ahead.

The past is an actuality. A pharaoh's tomb can provide a full story of his life and times. The future is not an abyss of the unknown. The progress of mankind is subject to sociological and economic laws governing the development of society. It can be assessed because of a factor which cannot be changed—the past. Past actions will produce results in the future. In the realm of economics, politics and thought certain whirlpools of force have been formed. Unless they are neutralised today, these vortices will sway the affairs of the future.

NOW is a point of union between two immeasurably long extensions—the past and the future. As John Quincy Adams wrote in the *Hour Glass*:

> Time was—Time shall be—drain the glass,
> But where in Time is NOW?

Past and future stretch backwards and forwards beyond the horizons of the cosmos.

What is this evasive instant called NOW? Is it a second? But one second is defined by science as a period of Time during which one of the elementary shells of caesium performs 9,192,631,770 oscillations. One oscillation seems to be an unimaginably small duration of Time but is it the end?

Atomic clocks measure Time with an accuracy of one second in three million years. Is this infinitesimal fraction of the second, or 10^{-14} the final NOW? But further subdivision is theoretically possible.

In its encounter with the future the present possesses extraordinary realism. But the nature of the present is no more real than the character of the future. Every tomorrow will become today. Every today is transformed into yesterday. The present is like the torch of a Marathon runner which is passed from one man to the next.

> Tomorrow and tomorrow and tomorrow,
> Creeps in this petty pace from day to day,
> To the last syllable of recorded time;
> And all our yesterdays have lighted fools
> The way to dusty death. Out, out, brief candle!
> Life's but a walking shadow . . .*

Shall we agree with Shakespeare that life is a walking shadow? If yesterday and tomorrow have no reality then he is right. But paleontology traces man to his ape-like infancy. Archaeology restores the life in ancient Egypt.

It is certain that by the process of mutation man will ultimately reach a higher stage in evolution. The past as well as future history of mankind exists now.

If the actuality of the present moment is made less intense, our Time range will broaden. This is exactly what happens in dreams in which one sees episodes of the past or incidents of a possible future.

*Macbeth, V, 5.

39

Dr. Alexis Carrel wrote in *Man the Unknown* that clairvoyants "perceive events which have already happened or which will take place in the future." He adds that they are sometimes incapable of distinguishing the past from the future.

According to Dr. J. B. Rhine extra-sensory perception is a faculty which affords freedom from the limitations of Time.

Rudyard Kipling had a precognitive dream about a ceremony at Westminster Abbey which he had not expected to attend. Six weeks later it was fulfilled in minute detail. The experience left him puzzled and he asked in *Something of Myself*: "How, and why, had I been shown an unreleased roll of my life-film?"

It is only when we are awake and conscious of the objective world that the Time Barrier manifests itself so strongly. Without this self-imposed limitation, Time would not be focused exclusively on the NOW.

Yesterday is but a today that is blotted out. In our memories events of the past can be reviewed with dramatic reality.

Tomorrow is but another today. With determination and imagination, one can plan it. Nevertheless, there is an element of probability in the future. But, all the same, the next chapter of one's life is already in the Book of Time.

The printed calendar contains 365 days, only one of which is today. A number of days and months belong to the past and some to the future. However, the days that have been lived and those which have not, are in the calendar.

The present is real only if viewed as a portion of the Time axis, containing past, present and future. Life is a constant flow of being into non-being. What is solid and tangible today will turn into dust tomorrow. But on the other hand, what does not yet exist, will eventually come into being. As Bhagavad Gita says, "good is the intellect which comprehends the coming forth and going back of life."

Heraclitus, the wise Greek of antiquity, said: "One and the same creature is alive and dead, awake and asleep, young and old." All that is and all that is not, being and non-being, are united in the relationship of one to the other, or becoming. Everything in the universe is changeable and transitory except the law of change.

Apollonius of Tyana brilliantly expounded this cosmic law in a letter to Consul Valerius: "There is no death of anyone but only in appearance even as there is no birth of any save only in seeming. The change from being to becoming seems to be birth and the change from becoming to being seems to be death, but in reality no one is ever born nor does one ever die. It is simply a being visible and then invisible: the former through the density of matter, and the latter because of the subtlety of being—being which is ever the same, its only change being motion and rest."

NOW seems to be the only real point in the Time dimension. Yet it is possible to evade its power whilst seeing an historical film from the life of ancient Egypt. A science fiction film like 2001—A Space Odyssey can take one out of the present. These are voyages in Time, created artificially.

Under the influence of narcotics people can lose all sense of Time. Happenings are either accelerated without the person being aware of it, or slowed down to the state of a frozen world. A similar incorrect estimation of Time is occasionally felt by the insane. A mentally deranged Russian woman has thus related her experience of a Time dilation: "Everything seemed dead. The whole world stood still. People move too slowly. Time has stopped. I know that the hour hand moves on your clocks but this is only an appearance of motion. You come to me from another Time."*

These lines look like a quotation from a science-fiction story rather than an extract from a medical report.

In another case, a patient experienced a diametrically opposite realisation of Time—the acceleration was equal to ten times the actual lapse, and six seconds were taken for sixty by the psychopath.

It is not necessary to use drugs or go mad in order to step out of the present. Perhaps a more natural way has been achieved by the mystics in their spiritual sublimation and ascent to a plane where the Time Barrier does not exist.

The Time Barrier is a limitation which separates the present from the past and the future. But the present has its roots in the past and holds the seeds of the future. Time makes sense only if taken in its entirety.

Space has three co-ordinates—width, depth and height. Destroy one of these and we are on Flatland. Remove another dimension, and we are in a one-dimensional world —a line.

We have reduced Time by one-third of its full meaning, at the expense of past and future. Man has focused his attention on the present instant and lost the significance of Time as a whole.

This is how Gautama the Buddha defined the present: "Just as a chariot wheel rolls only at one point of the tyre, and in resting rests only at one point, in the same way, the life of a living being lasts only for the period of one thought." But Time as a whole is the wheel.

With the awareness of the meaning of Time as Eternity, man will walk fast towards his goal—cosmic consciousness which would bring his mentality to a plane corresponding

*A. A. Leonov and V. I. Lebedev, *Cognition of Distance and Time in Space*, Moscow, 1968 (Russian).

to the Space Age. Perhaps he will then pierce the Time Barrier as William Blake who wrote these words: "I see the past, present and future existing all at once before me."

We are not today what we were yesterday. We have had many selves. If the self filled only the present moment, it would not be able to look forward or backward. A self limited by the present would neither be capable of storing experiences nor of learning. A self not aspiring to the future would lead a purposeless existence. The present self is only the projected part of the greater Time-transcending self.

Zoroaster said that the wise remember the past and understand the future but the ignorant live only for the fleeting pleasures of the present. Forgetting the past and not caring about the future creates an irresponsible attitude towards posterity.

The Australian aborigine is probably the only Earth-dweller who has solved the problem of Time. Whether his solution is right or wrong—is a different matter. To the aborigine of Australia events do not exist BEFORE or AFTER, they are all here at once. In his *Dreamtime* past, present and future co-exist. In tribal initiations the Australian has a glimpse of this eternal NOW-HERE.

10. CHANCE OR FATE?

EVER SINCE MAN began to think about his destiny, confronted by the forces of nature and survival for existence, a superstition developed whereby that he was merely a toy in the hands of some vengeful gods who had to be appeased.

On the other hand, the ancient Greeks in their speculation in the forums and academies entertained the idea that man was free.

This debate—Chance or Fate?—has never been conclusively won by either side, nor has it ended. It is still raging in the domain of science in the two opposing schools of cosmology—the Big Bang Theory versus the Steady State Theory.

Reichenbach wrote that "the morrow has already occurred today in the same sense as yesterday has." Bondi argues that "the passage of Time transforms statistical expectation into real events." But Reichenbach retorts: "Only the totality of all causes permits an inference concerning the future."

Because the future is uncertain and the past has disappeared, some thinkers have inferred that the present has no reality at all. It is said that Shankara, the teacher of Advaita Vedanta, who taught that the world is only an illusion, was present at a parade in India one day. As an elephant charged into a crowd, Shankara ran behind a tree. "Why do you run from the mere appearance of an elephant?" sarcastically asked a man. "I only appear to run," replied the philosopher.

In a true cosmic perspective, the present is real but no more so than the past or future. While the three divisions of Time are relative if taken independently, their totality is of an absolute nature.

It is not necessary to believe in predestination to say that the solar system will come to an end in a few milliard years. One does not have to be a determinist to state that the world of the year 12000 will be unrecognisable. These conclusions can be drawn from astronomy and history.

It is not fatalism to declare that "I shall not live to the age of one hundred and fifty." This deduction is made on the basis of the average mortality limit. Nevertheless, an unforeseen factor should not be overlooked even in this reasonable assumption. Although one hundred and fifty is an unusual age to reach, hypothetically a man could live to that age if he had a membership card of the Life Extension Society of America. The slogan of the organisation is "Freeze, wait and reanimate." If this hibernation is perfected, one may indeed be able to jump into later century.

Nowadays scientists believe that the smallest units of matter follow laws which can only be described as probabilities. In physics every forecast demands the inclusion of an unpredictable chance.

According to Laplace "the probability of an event is the ratio of the number of cases which favour it to the number of all possible cases, when nothing leads us to believe that one of these cases ought to occur rather than the others, which renders them, for us, equally possible."

The mathematical theory of probability is well exemplified by games of chance. In the game of heads or tails, the chance of heads coming up is one in two, but it is impossible to predict what it will be on the next toss. It would be an amazing feat for anyone to throw fifty heads in succession. In fact, it is much more amazing than one might think—to accomplish this, a coin would have to be thrown continuously for two hundred million years, or the time it takes our galaxy to turn once on its axis!

The science of probability regards all future events as mere probabilities and only measures their degree of realisation.

Foreordained future or pure accident? But perhaps the question can not be posed so sharply. Science is full of paradoxes.

Freewill or fate? There is no doubt that a man or a nation has a considerable amount of freedom of action. But the course of action will be determined by tradition, environment and other factors, which limit a really free choice. Let us suppose a man has an opportunity in his life. His first consideration will centre on its advantages but this normal reaction will neutralise the exercise of freedom in choosing a road in life.

The epoch, country, family, inherited abilities and assets mark our "horoscopes" with beneficial or malefic signs and form the pattern of our lives. But there is wide scope for a man to ruin his assets or shed his liabilities.

When it comes to the physiological process of ageing, man has no freewill. Shakespeare plotted the course of man and described his seven ages. He starts "mewling and puking in the nurse's arms" and finishes up in "second childishness and mere oblivion, sans teeth, sans eyes, sans taste, sans everything."

Between childhood and old age there is a kaleidoscopic array of circumstances, some of which can be predicted with reasonable accuracy while others can not.

In the controversy between a free-future concept of Time and determinism, one should take the position of the golden mean.

Were the future determined, we could follow the path of a unit into Time and see its future. However, the law of necessity and the theory of probability must enter this observation and corrections must be made on the apparent course.

Strictly speaking, it is not determinism to say that there are certain goals in the future but the roads to them are many.

Strange as it seems, the two opposing ideologies of the world today are determinist to a large extent. Religion teaches about the inevitability of the second coming of Christ, the advent of a Messiah, Mahdi, Kalki Avatar and Maitreya Buddha. On the other hand, the historical materialism of Marx affirms that as the primitive communal society was replaced by slavery, slavery by feudalism, feudalism by capitalism—so will capitalism be replaced by socialism. In Marxism this change of systems is an inevitable law.

There is a wide difference between a scientific or religious determinism and a belief in a fixed destiny which none can avoid. What makes man accomplish anything in this world is his freewill. Shakespeare understood the privilege of man to act freely when he said: "The fault, dear Brutus, is not in our stars but in ourselves that we are underlings."

In spite of the pressure of circumstances, man creates his destiny every moment of his life.

11. TIME TELEVISION

IN THE 19TH CENTURY the French Academy of Sciences did not accept claims for projects of a tunnel under the English Channel and designs of piloted balloons. The restrictions have been lifted but probably new ones substituted instead. Time Rockets, Time Machines and Time Television may be on that list.

The topic of Time Machines has stirred the imagination of writers. H. G. Wells is his *Time Machine* describes how his hero succeeded in building one. The projectile flew into the future where the man saw a golden age. Then aeons later he observed scenes of our dying planet. After this exploration of the future the character in the story was returned to the present.

A *Chronobile* is the subject of a Russian novel by Nikolsky, *A Thousand Years Later*. His *Time Ship* is spherical and contains a meter. When the indicator turns to the left, the machine travels into the past. If the arrow points to the right, the chronobile flies towards the future.

Unlike Jules Verne's *From the Earth to the Moon*

which inspired Tsiolkovsky and Oberth in their space rocketry work, Time-Machine fiction has not stimulated any inventors.

However, Emile Drouet, a French engineer and astronomer, has attempted to build a rocket to fly into the past. Emile Drouet displayed his *Time Rocket* at Vigneux-sur-Seine in 1946. Manipulating with complicated mathematical formulas, Drouet writes in his bulky project that: "One must admit that in a few centuries or millennia, voyages in Time will become a reality and a practical possibility."*

In its spin the Earth travels around the sun at the speed of 107,181 kilometres per hour. The whole solar system flies through space towards the constellation of Hercules to a point near Vega at the velocity of 69,198 kilometres per hour. As the Earth revolves around the sun and moves in interstellar space, it traces a spiral.

Like most scientists, Drouet regards Time as static: Time stays—we move. To travel back to the past it is necessary to re-trace our steps and find the exact spot where the Earth was in space at a specific date. This voyage in Time is without return and man would have to be replaced by machines.

The technique of this Time travel is simple from the theoretical standpoint. Compare the spiral track of our planet's flight through space with a spring from your old bed mattress, and have a pencil ready. Let us put the spring on the carpet and agree that this is the course of our Earth in space, with each coil symbolising one orbit around the sun. In temporal sense, the spring will take us as many years back as there are coils. Bring the pencil to the spring so that it will touch all the coils on the outside at any point. That is the course of Drouet's Rocket, from the top coil to the bottom one. Instead of travelling down

*R. Charroux, *Histoire Inconnue des Hommes*, Paris, 1963.

the spiral, the rocket flies downward by a short cut and the pencil is the track of that rocket.

Drouet's Rocket is launched perpendicularly to the ecliptic and away from the point in space towards which the solar system is moving.

The speed of the spacecraft should be equivalent to the velocity of the Earth in its journey around the sun, or approximately 107,000 kilometres per hour. Drouet's *Time Spaceship* is equipped with gyroscopes, radar and innumerable other gear.

If the rocket were launched in 1973 and is supposed to reach the year of the French Revolution, it would have to touch 184 coils or rings of the spiral path of the Earth in space in order to find the point where our planet was in 1789. When, and if, the spaceship reaches that spot in interstellar space, instruments will begin to amplify the pictures of the Earth at that date, showing scenes of the French Revolution. These events will be relayed to the Earth at its present position. Such is a brief, non-technical content of Emile Drouet's fantastic project.

The practical realisation of this Time Probe would be costly and difficult. From the relativist viewpoint, motion in space does not imply motion into the past. Daring as the project is, its theoretical basis is not faultless.

Had anyone predicted a hundred years ago that a box with a glass screen would show living pictures of an earthquake in Sicily or of warfare in Vietnam to observers in Paris or New York at the very time the events were taking place, he would have been certified insane. Yet nowadays we watch our television nightly and think nothing of it. Television has become one of the many electrical appliances that we have adopted.

Perhaps in a century or less, Time will be mastered and scenes of a distant past will unfold before our eyes on a Time Television screen. And, who knows, we may be able to see things to come in giant television computers.

As long ago as the thirties, the American philosopher Manly P. Hall wrote about the Time Viewing Machine: "Though the past sinks into shadows which our physical senses cannot penetrate, it nevertheless still exists, and if its vibrations be intensified by electrical amplification, the ages can be made to live again. At our pleasure, we could, by turning a little dial, watch the pyramid builders heaping mountains of granite together; once more would senators argue in the Roman Forum; the lurid flames of the Inquisition would burn before our eyes, to be followed by the firebrands of the French Revolution."*

There are not too many scientists in the world today who can draw a red line beyond which would lie the impossible. Science has progressed so much in the last half-century that all the impossibilities of the 19th century have become commonplace things in this age of Science. The most fantastic ideas of today, such as Time Television, may be materialised tomorrow.

The over-cautious professors of this century should bear in mind the underestimations and errors of their colleagues of the past. The famous physicist Poincaré once said: "It is impossible to destroy a city with a kilo of metal." But he was wrong—a few kilogrammes of uranium were sufficient to destroy Hiroshima.

Scepticism can be extremely costly. An American engineer came to the Tuileries in 1807 and asked to see Napoleon I. He was announced as Robert Fulton by the palace marshal. In his hand Mr. Fulton carried a roll of drawings showing how steam engines could be installed in French Navy ships, in order to defeat England.

"Only yesterday I received a project to attack the English coast by means of cavalry carried on the backs of

*M. P. Hall, *The Mystery of Electricity*, Los Angeles, 1929.

dolphins. Go away! You are one of those madmen," exclaimed the Emperor.

Eight years later the English sailing vessel *Bellerophon* was taking the captive conqueror to St. Helena. In the open sea the faster American steamer *Fulton* overtook the British ship.

"For having chased Fulton from the Tuileries I lost my crown!" sadly said Napoleon Bonaparte to his companion Bertrand.

The steamship seemed a madman's dream a century and a half ago. Time Television is in exactly the same position today.

Can past events be photographed after they have occurred? At first the question may seem absurd. But an Associated Press report of August 17, 1958 released via the *Miami Herald*, described earth-shaking experiments which the United States Air Force was carrying out at that time.

A special infra-red camera photographed an empty parking lot from a reconnaissance plane. The result was a photograph of cars which had been parked on the lot several hours previously, and which were not there at the time the pictures were taken.

Test officials at Eglin Air Force Base in Florida explained that the film of the wonder-camera was sensitive to heat rays, emitted by solid objects, instead of light rays as in the case of an ordinary camera This extremely sensitive equipment can distinguish, in thousandths of a degree, heat contrasts between objects and their background. The greater the contrast, the clearer the photograph.

Because of the classified nature of the infra-red photographic camera, the U.S. Air Force did not disclose how far backward into time a picture could be taken. The officials did not release their "time pictures" to the public for fear that trained scientists in other countries might have "read too much from them."

To take a snapshot of empty space and see one's car on the photograph at a spot where it was two hours ago, is truly breaking the Barrier of Time.

On rare occasions radio and television pick up programmes broadcast at a previous time. Delayed reception due to reflection from ionised layers could explain this time displacement.

But here is a case that might be a demonstration of *Time Televising*. In September 1954 Mrs. John Mackey of Indianapolis, Indiana, was astounded to see her dead grandfather George Shots on her television. The image "froze" on the screen, showed no matter whether the set was on or off, and could not be wiped away.

After watching the "ghost image" hundreds of electronic experts and detectives tried to solve the mystery without giving the ultimate answer to the riddle.*

A Time Viewing Machine is possible provided atoms record all changes in the physical world. The British scientist Arthur Clarke conjectures that all events may leave some mark upon the universe at a level which our instruments cannot yet reach.†

Isaac Asimov in his science fiction story *The Dead Past* writes about a man who invented a neutrino recorder and learned how to interpret the pattern of neutrino stream. His idea is that in its continuous passage through matter the stream is affected and deflected by it. These deflections can be converted into images of the matter that has done the deflecting, thus making Time Viewing possible.

Can the atom react to human thought? The answer is, yes. Professor Rémy Chauvin of Strasbourg University used an isotope of uranium, a Geiger counter and thought power in a series of unearthly experiments. The counter was automatically stopped every minute and the experi-

Daily Telegraph, Sydney, September 14, 1954.
†A. C. Clarke, *Profiles of the Future*, New York, 1960.

mentators were asked to will with their minds that the radioactive disintegration be accelerated the first minute and slowed down during the second. In the course of the third minute the experimentators did nothing to influence mentally the process of isotopic disintegration.

When the results were checked, the Professor and his assistants could not believe their eyes! The human mind could control the rate of isotopic disintegration. For fifteen days the experiments were repeated the experimentators changed, and the findings were the same. "These experiments have certainly surprised us," said Professor Chauvin in Moscow.*

The tests were then taken over by the physicists who used the most modern counters and radioactive strontium instead of uranium isotopes. Their experiments produced the same results—mind can influence atomic processes. It follows that the atom may be sensitive to our mental radiations.

One wonders if cheaper methods of building a Time Television set were known to the ancients. A study of ancient folklore discloses the presence of *Magic Mirrors* in bygone epochs.

A description of such a mirror constructed in Tibet might be of some help to an imaginative scientist experimenting with Time Machines:

"Every temple has a dark room, the north wall of which is entirely covered with a sheet of mixed metal, chiefly copper, very highly polished, with a surface capable of reflecting things, as distinctly as a mirror. The chela (disciple) sits on an insulated seat, a three-legged stool placed in a flat-bottomed vessel of thick glass, the lama operator likewise, the two forming a triangle with the mirror wall. A magnet with the north pole up

*Znanie-Sila magazine, No. 9, 1967 (U.S.S.R.).

suspended over the crown of the chela's head without touching it. The operator, having started the thing going, leaves the chela alone gazing at the wall, and after the third time he is no longer required."*

It is said that three-dimensional Time pictures are seen by the lamas in this *Magic Mirror*.

A friend of mine has actually seen scenes of the future on an even less sophisticated Time Television screen. He was a Russian emigré employed by the Chinese Eastern Railway in Manchuria in the nineteen-twenties. On one of his inspection tours he visited a small station located amidst hills and forests. There he met an old Chinese jen-seng root prospector engaged in the search for this rare medicinal root, prized by the Chinese as the elixir of life.

In the course of their conversation the old Taoist expressed his admiration for Western science, at the same time making a sly remark to the effect that the East also possessed a science of its own, just as efficient as that of the West.

"Give me your handkerchief, please," the old herbalist said. As my friend complied with this request, the Taoist unfolded the handkerchief before him. "Now look at your handkerchief," the Chinaman said to my friend on that memorable sunny day in Manchuria. All of a sudden pictures began to appear on the handkerchief, as if on a miniature cinema screen. There were battles between soldiers dressed in Japanese and Chinese uniforms. Then he saw himself travelling to a warmer region of China. As hundreds of scenes flashed before my friend's eyes, he could discern terrible war action scenes with bombings and artillery bombardment. More frames of this Time motion picture—and he caught sight of himself on a long voyage and then the last chapter of his life.

Mahatma Letters, London, 1926.

The most astonishing feature of this experience was that the man actually watched on his handkerchief—the occupation of Manchuria by Japan, his subsequent life in Shanghai, World War II in the Pacific, his eventual departure for Europe when I lost track of him. This episode indirectly supports the hypothesis that Time Television is a scientific possibility.

Once upon a time in ancient Greece a girl sat in front of a mirror and combed her long hair in the dark of the night. Every time she touched her hair with the amber comb, sparks flew. In the Middle Ages an old woman sitting by the fire stroked her cat's fur and heard crackling. This is all that Benjamin Franklin had to work with before he flew his kite and brought down lightning from the sky. If it were not for that amber comb and that cat, we might not have electricity today. The moral being—just a few seemingly unimportant facts can lead to a great discovery.

Before this century history gave us but ten per cent of all the scientists who ever lived. The rest—ninety per cent —are alive today. What are they doing about Time Television? Let us be patient—difficult things take time but the impossible takes a little longer.

12. EXPERIMENTS WITH TIME

THERE IS NO BETTER method to prove a theory than by testing it. First of all, let us assume that this moment of Time and yourself are real. Look around, observe all the objects and hear all the sounds. This is the first step in experimentation with Time—to feel that NOW is real.

The next step is to do something special on one day. It does not matter exactly what it is, as long as it is remembered clearly—for instance, it might be anything from a concert to a football game. While there, study everything in your range of vision and then try to take a Time motion picture in the course of a few seconds or minutes, registering all that it is possible to see and hear in your immediate surroundings. At the same time, sense the utmost reality of NOW-HERE.

A number of days or weeks later, bring yourself into a passive state to actualise how real this new place and time is. Now mentally project your psychological motion picture on the invisible screen of your mind—with all its details, colours and sounds. The scene is gone, yet it was not an illusion but reality as concrete as the moment at which you are now contemplating that past episode. This conclusion could easily be proved by playing back a tape-recording or projecting a movie, had you made one. For the human mind does register everything just like a tape recorder or camera.

When an event has a traumatic effect on the soul, the imprint will last for a long time to come. The memory of a war-time scene has haunted a friend of mine for decades. He can still see a bomb slowly dropping at an angle from under an enemy plane. Then a terrible explosion took place with concrete, brick and dust flying in the air. Severed limbs and dead bodies were scattered all around. He was the only spectator to that drama. It did not seem possible that, like a dream, it could ever vanish into oblivion.

After these experiments with Time, a realisation will come that the present is no more real than the past which you have left. By reviving the past, the Time Barrier can be broken.

The future seems to be a giant question mark facing us. Yet *something* will happen in that future. This conclusion alone presumes the reality of future. Now project yourself to a future event, expected to take place at some future date, such as a party or a vacation abroad. Draw a scenario of that future. When the happenings occur, even though they diverge from your original script, note the absolute reality of what is taking place. Then recall the day when you were only dreaming about the event—the day that will have become the past by now.

If the present is real, the future must have a reality of some kind even with its random element because something can produce only another something, never a nothing. So the future exists NOW in the Time dimension, even though the exact shape it will take is not certain.

Make an effort to regard the present, past and future as one reality, or as numerous frames of one whole motion picture reel. This reel exists NOW whether or not we project it on our mental screen.

A few experiments with Time can teach a better lesson than many arguments. The strange faculty of precognition, potentially present in all human beings, may unexpectedly manifest itself in the form of precognitive dreams, as a wider angle of temporal vision is developed by reducing the dominance of the present moment or NOW.

PART TWO

They broke the time barrier

---

13. FORETELLING BY GUESS OR ACCIDENT

SCIENCE CAN PROPHESY—for instance, a solar eclipse in the year 1999 can be predicted by mere mathematical calculation. In antiquity these scientific predictions were regarded as supernatural miracles. Thales of Miletus declared that there would be a total eclipse of the sun on May 28, 585 B.C. The Medes and Lydians were engaged in a battle on that day. When the sun blackened, they remembered the prophecy of Thales. The incident impressed the two armies so much that they signed a treaty for a lasting peace.

The feat of Thales ranks less in achievement in comparison with the long-range prophecies of friar Roger Bacon (1214-1292). Although the telescope was invented by Galileo and the microscope by Leeuwenhoek in the 17th century, Roger Bacon anticipated these discoveries in the 13th century. The learned monk, who was educated at the University of Paris and lectured at Oxford, left ciphered writings which contain farsighted predictions:

"It is possible to construct spying glasses by which the most distant objects can be drawn near to us so that we shall be able to read the most minute writing, at an almost incredible distance to see all kinds of diminutive objects and to make the stars appear whenever we chose."

There is no doubt that he foresaw the ocean liners of today: "Instruments may be made by which the largest ships, with only one man guiding them, will be carried with greater speed than if they were full of sailors."

Roger Bacon had a mental image of our cars, buses and trains when he wrote that "chariots may be constructed that will move with incredible rapidity without the help of animals."

Last but not least, he had given thought to building an aeroplane: "Machines for flying can be made in which a man sits and turns an ingenious device, by which skilfully contrived wings are made to strike the air, in the manner of a flying bird."

Speculation of this kind is quite extraordinary, especially when we compare it with the opinions held by some of our ancestors only a century ago.

An argument between a dean of an American college and a clergyman took place in 1875. The scholarly dean claimed that men would fly like birds in fifty years' time. "Only angels have the right to fly," angrily remarked the Reverend. The joke was on him—his sons Orville and Wilbur Wright, who were then four and eight years old— flew the first aeroplane twenty-eight years later.

Roger Bacon was quite right when he predicted that the development of science "will make all kinds of magic appear trivial and unworthy." His prophecies, made in the 13th century, have been fulfilled in our technological era.

Leonardo da Vinci (1452-1519) was another genius who proved the truthfulness of the formula "Intelligence plus Imagination equals Prophecy."

The Institut de France in Paris is in possession of manuscripts from the hand of the great Leonardo. The manuscript marked D clearly shows the wing of an aeroplane. The B manuscript depicts a helicopter and a study of the lifting power of an airship wing.

In his famous *Notebooks* one can find a suggestion of an aqualung or a diving suit: "How by means of a certain machine many people may stay some time under water." He tried to devise methods by which people could survive in a storm and invented an early *May West Jacket*—"a method of escaping in a tempest and shipwreck at sea," as he put it.

Leonardo did a tremendous amount of work on aerodynamics and discovered that "an object offers as much resistance to the air as the air does to the object." He must have envisaged our ways of communication such as the telephone, telegraph, radio and postal services: "Men will speak with each other from the most remote countries, and reply." It goes without saying that five hundred years ago all of these things were in the realm of fantasy.

History knows of incidents in which persons with greater knowledge benefited from their "prophecies" made to the ignorant. Christopher Columbus found himself and his landing party in dire circumstances in Jamaica when they ran short of food and the natives refused to feed the Spaniards.

Fortunately for the expedition, he recalled that, according to the astronomical calendar, a full eclipse of the moon was expected that night. The adventurous Columbus decided to play the role of an oracle and told the Indians that if he and his seamen were not fed, he could cover up the moon when night came. His prophetic utterances were ignored until the eclipse began. In no time ample provisions were provided by the frightened islanders.

The history of science is full of prophecies. The 19th-century astronomers Leverrier and Adams worked out by mathematics that there was another planet beyond Uranus. On September 23, 1846, Galle discovered Neptune from the Berlin Observatory at the exact point in the sky where Leverrier and Adams had estimated it should have been.

The English astronomer Edmund Halley studied the

appearance of comets in the years 1531, 1607 and 1682, and decided it was one and the same body. Before he died in 1742 Halley had written these words about the comet: "Hence I think I may venture to foretell that it will return again in the year 1758."

There was great excitement among the scholars when the year arrived. On Christmas Eve 1758 the comet was spotted by a farmer in Saxony. The prediction was verified and the comet became known as Halley's Comet.

Scientific prophecies are based on logic and the theory of probability. But there is a type of prophecy which can really be termed accidental.

On August 28, 1883, the *Boston Globe* featured an article by a young reporter Byron Somes on its front page. It vividly described an exploding island in the Indonesian archipelago. After a tremendous eruption of volcanoes, the island vanished in the sea.

It took weeks and months before detailed accounts of the destruction of Krakatoa, between Java and Sumatra, on August 26-28, 1883, began to arrive by slow sea mail, to confirm the story by Somes. This scoop in journalism was uncannily accurate in its details. In fact, when the story appeared in America, the Krakatoa volcano was still exploding in what is known as the greatest geological disaster of all times. The volcano released energy now estimated to have been a million times greater than the explosion of a hydrogen-bomb.

From the meagre dispatches from Batavia of earlier eruptions, Byron Somes intuitively sensed the magnitude of the catastrophes and by consulting a public library built up the story. This "prophecy" had almost cost him his career, until it was verified.

The *Argosy Magazine* had a story *The Blood-Red Haze of Madness* by Osborne in 1904. It described the Earth as drifting through a crimson haze which turned Earthlings into mad killers. In the plot a man jumped from a window shouting "Beware of 1914". The passing of the Earth through the tail of Halley's Comet in 1910 and the beginning of World War I in 1914, are suggested by this prophetic story.

As if this fulfilled prophecy were not enough, another magazine in the U.S.A. re-published the same story in 1928 with a slight change—the man in the tale shrieked "Beware of 1941". In June 1941 Nazi Germany attacked Russia and in December of the same year Japan bombed Pearl Harbor, setting the world aflame again. The story scored two direct hits.

In its May 1, 1912, issue, *Popular Magazine* printed a story by Mayn Garnett about the maiden voyage of the largest ocean liner in the world. Near Newfoundland an iceberg ripped through her bottom, creating one of the greatest shipwrecks in history. Seven days after the magazine was first displayed on news-stands on April 7, the P. & O. *Titanic*, the giant "unsinkable" steamship, was sunk by an iceberg in the North Atlantic, exactly as the story said.

Morgan Robertson, an English author, did even better than Garnett—he had predicted the shipwreck of *Titanic* fourteen years before it actually took place.

In 1898 Mansfield of London published his novel *Futility* about a huge Transatlantic liner *Titan*—the fastest and the most luxurious steamer in the world. In this story *Titan* hits an iceberg and sinks with its hundreds of rich passengers on its maiden voyage. According to Robertson this takes place one cold night in April.

This is an amazing coincidental prediction as the name of the ship *Titan* is almost identical with that of the *Titanic* which sank in the month of April. There are other correspondences—*Titan* had four funnels and three screws. So did *Titanic*. The length of the fictional ship was 260 metres and 268 in actual life. The tonnage and the engine power were almost the same, too. The top speed of *Titan* was given by Morgan Robertson as 25 knots. Such likewise was the speed of the *Titanic*.

To these curious cases of accidental prediction should be added the verse of the Russian poet André Bely written in 1919:

> *In an experiment of Curie,*
> *The atom-bomb exploded in a fury.*

A year after World War I only a prophet could have foreseen a future nuclear weapon. Even Rutherford and Einstein discounted this ghastly possibility at the time.

In 1927 another Russian writer—V. Nikolsky—in his novel *A Thousand Years Later*, correctly predicted the date of the first atomic explosion—1945.

The story *Solution Unsatisfactory* by the famous science-fiction writer Robert Heinlein describes an Uranium-235 atom-bomb which was dropped by the United States on an enemy's city in the closing stages of World War II. The Federal Bureau of Investigation accused the author of "disclosing top military secrets." But he was soon acquitted because Heinlein's book was published in 1941, or four years before the atomic bombing of Hiroshima.

14. TIME RECORDINGS

PROFESSOR IVAN EFREMOV has made a proposal to establish a scientific institute for pooling "mad ideas". Scientists and science fiction writers would be able to meet at this

© Lorillard 1975

C'mon

Come for the filter. **You'll stay for the taste.**

19 mg. "tar," 1.2 mg. nicotine av. per cigarette, FTC Report Apr. '75.

Warning: The Surgeon General Has Determined That Cigarette Smoking Is Dangerous to Your Health.

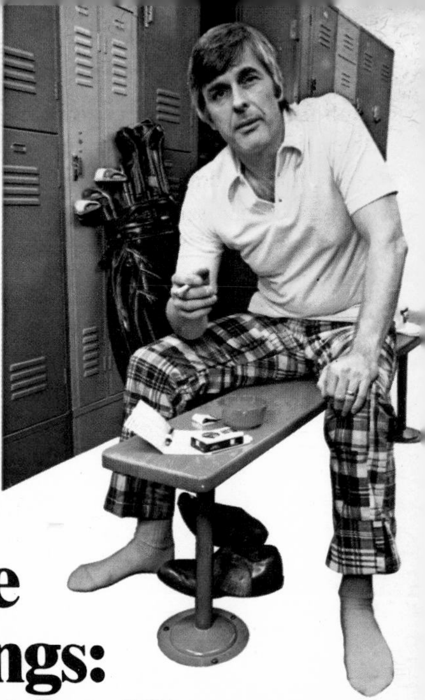

I'd heard enough to make me decide one of two things: quit or smoke True.

I smoke True.

**The low tar, low nicotine cigarette.
Think about it.**

King Regular: 11 mg. "tar", 0.6 mg. nicotine, King Menthol: 12 mg. "tar", 0.7 mg. nicotine, 100's Regular: 13 mg. "tar", 0.7 mg. nicotine, 100's Menthol: 13 mg. "tar", 0.8 mg. nicotine, av. per cigarette, FTC Report April '75.

Warning: The Surgeon General Has Determined That Cigarette Smoking Is Dangerous to Your Health.

club for the exchange of new ideas and perhaps to convert them into discoveries and inventions. The professor does not intend to create another debating society or a workshop of newspaper sensations. He believes that many theories on the fringe of the impossible can be realised.

In his novel *The Razor's Edge* Efremov raises a fantastic possibility. Do our cells contain Time recordings of the former experience of our innumerable ancestors?

He writes that the human organism carries the accumulated experience of numerous generations from the caveman to the astronaut. Potentially, the body cells contain the memory of existence in the dim past. These physiologically stored reminiscences occasionally cause a certain type of hallucination. This suggests a breathtaking possibility of the cell memory with recording for millions of years.

If a normal mind is split into the conscious and subconscious spheres, untapped resources of information, containing the imprints of thousands of generations, will be opened to man. When this subconscious memory is reflected in the conscious mind, the brain may be able to decode this information.

By means of electrical stimulation of certain areas of the brain Dr. G. Penfield of Canada has split the human personality in two. In this test one half of the individual has awareness of the present while the other is completely transferred into the past. What is more, the "I" of today is able to act in the life of yesterday! In one experiment the scientist asked a patient to count the number of bricks in a brick wall which formed the backdrop of a past scene. The number given by the patient was found to be correct later, as the wall is still intact. It appears that the normal person is continuously balancing his "I remember" with his "I forgot". But nothing is really forgotten and the past can be made alive by electrical stimulation of the brain or hypnosis.

Professor Ivan Efremov refers to reincarnation which he, as a materialist, cannot accept and writes that the transfer of Time-recorded hereditary traits, from one individual to another in an unbroken line from prehistoric man, constitutes true immortality of the species.

The scientist says that cybernetics has enabled science to create a concept of the workings of the brain. A programmed cell in a computer can be compared with the body cell. Theoretically, flashes of the life of our distant ancestors can appear before our gaze. They are the "hallucinations" he speaks about.

15. PROJECTION INTO THE PAST AND FUTURE

THERE ARE MANY things which cannot be accepted by our minds even if they are true. Lack of facts is not always the explanation. A consciousness constrained by dogma and authority is often unable to see the truth.

Today we depend so much on science. But a great deal of what was scientific in physics one hundred years ago is unscientific today. On the other hand, most of the accepted scientific conclusions of this century would have been rejected by the professors a century ago. It can, therefore, be assumed that what is "unscientific" at present may be quite legitimate in a few decades from now. The relativity of knowledge is supported by history. The growth of science is a process of discarding fallacies.

Tsiolkovsky once said to a fellow scientist: "The bolder the idea opening an unexpected future perspective, the more violent the reaction from obscurants who conveniently take cover behind science."

In Part One important scientific views were expressed to the effect that Time is relative and dependent upon the point of observation. It was explained how Time could shrink in a space rocket propelled by photon or antimatter fuel. It was also shown that the Arrow of Time, pointing from the past to the future in our world, is not turned in the same direction in the antiworld. Time direction can be reversed, says science, and past and future have their own reality. Consequently, it may well be that the Time Barrier, which separates them, is not so impregnable as it is generally believed to be.

In his cell in the Schliesselburg Fortress a Russian revolutionary, N. A. Morozov, wrote about Time in 1891: "If instead of being drifted towards unknown horizons by the uniform current of Time we could travel on it—into the past or the future as we chose, then Time would appear only as a dimension, exactly as height, depth or thickness."

The present is built on the rock of the past. The past, therefore, can not be unreal because reality cannot emerge out of unreality, any more than something out of nothing. The memories of yesterday are as tangible as the experiences of today.

It is easy to prove that there is no absolute present. Let us suppose that there is a high civilisation in the system of the star Deneb, 400 light years away from the Earth. If Deneb's technology is advanced enough to magnify what they see through their telescopes, the Denebians would study the Earth as it was in the time of Queen Elizabeth I. The scenes of England would not be a mere cliché of historical events but an actual panorama of life in the 16th century.

This example serves to show that it is theoretically possible to observe the past in all its reality. Can we see the past without instrumentation?

Ever since the days of the prophets who correctly foretold the future, there has ever lurked a suspicion in the human mind that the five senses are not the limits of our powers of perception.

We are all flying into the future at the rate of 24 hours a day. But seers are able to decelerate or accelerate this speed and make excursions into the bygone past or the unknown future.

Retrocognition or precognition are phases of para-psychological phenomenon. Scientific institutions of such high standing as Duke University, Cornell University, Cambridge and Leningrad University study this branch of science.

According to G. N. M. Tyrrell retrocognition is "non-inferential knowledge of past events outside the range of the subject's memory."[*]

In his book *Clairvoyance* C. W. Leadbeater thus describes the manifestation of *psi* in travelling into the past, say for instance, a seer watching an autumn morning in the year 55 B.C. when Julius Caesar landed in England: "He finds himself not looking at any picture but standing on the shore among the legionaries with the whole scene being enacted around him."[†]

In this stepping into the past, the actors of the scene are entirely unconscious of the observer because he lives in their future. But the person able to use this faculty in watching the past "can control the rate at which the drama shall pass before him—can have the events of the whole year unfold before his eyes in a single hour, or can at any moment stop the movement altogether, and hold any particular scene in view, as a picture, as long as he chooses."

Precognition or non-inferential knowledge of future events is more baffling than retrocognition, the awareness

[*]G. N. M. Tyrrell, *The Personality of Man*, London, 1948.
[†]C. W. Leadbeater, *Clairvoyance*, Adyar, 1939.

of the past. Dr. J. B. Rhine, the distinguished American scientist who pioneered ESP research, writes: "If the human mind can actually leap the boundaries of Time and report on things that have not yet happened, the discovery of that fact should bring about a major revolution in the concept of man and the universe."*

Is there such a faculty dormant in the human mind? History testifies to its reality. Herodotus recounts many historical prophecies given by the Oracles.

King Croesus had a son who was dumb and nothing could be done to restore his speech. When the Delphic Oracle was consulted by the king, the priestess replied:

O Lydian lord of many nations, foolish Croesus,
Wish not to hear the longed-for voice within your palace,
Even your son's voice: better for you were it otherwise;
For his first word will he speak on a day of sorrow.

When Croesus lost the war with the Persians, an enemy soldier was about to cut him down. But his dumb son, seeing the danger, was so terrified that he broke into speech and shouted: "Do not kill Croesus!"

After the capture of Sardis, Croesus was taken prisoner but his son retained the power of speech for the rest of his life, gained on so sad a day, exactly as the Oracle predicted.

The exiled prince of Egypt Psammetichus sent for advice to the Oracle of Buto. The priests prophesied that help would come from the sea from "bronze men". Psammetichus did not understand the prophecy. But not long afterwards it so happened that Greek sea raiders, forced by bad weather, landed on Egyptian soil. They were clad in bronze armour. When Psammetichus found out about this landing of the "bronze men", he recruited them into his forces. With the help of the Greek warriors he attacked

*'Do Dreams Come True?' *Reader's Digest*, April, 1955.

the eleven princes who had exiled him and then became master of Egypt.

The Oracle of Heliopolis in Egypt had a great fame in antiquity. Before starting a war with the Parthians the Roman Emperor Trajan, who ruled between 98 and 117 A.D., sent messengers to consult this Oracle. The hierophants gave no verbal or written reply but handed only a broken branch. Trajan died in the campaign and his body was brought to Rome.

When Spurinna Vestritius, a holy man of ancient Rome, told Julius Caesar to beware of the Ides of March, the conqueror only grinned. And when on the fateful day of March 15, 44 B.C., Caesar met Spurinna on the way to the Senate, he shouted jokingly: "Well, the Ides of March are here and there is nothing happening." "Yes, Caesar, they are here but not yet over," replied the augur. The tragic end of Julius Caesar confirmed the prediction given as a warning.

When a seer predicted to Prince Oleg of ancient Russia that his favourite steed would be the cause of his death, he sent the horse away. Five years later, in the year 912 A.D., he expressed the wish to see the body of the horse which had died some time previously. When he arrived to examine the skeleton of the steed, from the skull issued a snake which inflicted on the Prince's foot a mortal sting.

According to the testimony of the Marquis de Launey, the governor of the Bastille, given to the revolutionary tribunal, Count Cagliostro carved the following inscription on the wall of his cell in the Bastille before the French Revolution: "Peace to the people of France. On the fourteenth of July, 1789, this Bastille will be destroyed by you and grass will grow where it now stands." The fourteenth of July is now the French national holiday commemorating the taking of the Bastille, predicted so accurately by the occultist.

One of the most celebrated predictions as to the downfall of the Bourbons belongs also to Count Cagliostro delivered in a Masonic Lodge in Paris in 1785: "Louis XVI will ruin the throne of his ancestors and he will die on the scaffold in the thirty-ninth year of his age."*

Cardinal Pierre d'Ailly of Paris made a startling prophecy of the French Revolution four hundred years before its outbreak.

Madame Le Normand had given Joachim Murat, then King of Naples, a card reading. She frankly told him that execution awaited him. On insistence from the disconcerted king, the cards were laid three times, each time with the same result. The prediction was fulfilled as Murat met his fate by military execution in Calabria in 1816.

To Bernadotte, another of Napoleon's generals, she promised a kingdom far away. The forecast came true as Bernadotte received the crown of Sweden and Norway. His descendant rules Sweden today.

To Napoleon III at the height of his pomp Baha-Ullah sent the following message: "Thy doings shall throw thy kingdom into confusion, sovereignty shall pass from thy hands." This was fulfilled two years later, when the French Emperor was defeated by Prussia in 1871 and lost his crown.

In an address delivered in California in 1912 Baha-Ullah said "two years hence only a spark will set aflame the whole of Europe." World War I broke out in 1914 as he forecast.

"The scientist should expect that any power of the mind that is not hemmed in by space would not be bound by Time either," writes Professor Rhine.†

The work of Rhine, Soal, Myers, Carington, Hettinger and others has provided enough evidence for the acceptance of precognition by the academic world.

*H. J. Forman, *The Story of Prophecy*, New York, 1936.
†'Do Dreams Come True?' *Reader's Digest*, April, 1955.

"I believe that the time is drawing near when it will be possible to suggest a systematic exploration of the future," wrote H. G. Wells in *The Discovery of the Future*.

If reports of precognitive visions of the future of the world were collected on a global scale, a picture of the possible future could be constructed. If it were not for the difficulties in programming, a computer could also do that.

H. G. Wells believed that man is able to accelerate his drift in the Time dimension. Tradition of all peoples has recorded the lives and deeds of seers who were able to foretell the future. But to find cases of authentic gifts of prophecy is like hunting for a diamond in a heap of stones. Naturally, the evidence should be strong enough not to be explained away as coincidence.

Wells wrote that we are inclined to overestimate the certainty of the past and underestimate the certainty of the future. He did not think that the future was a perpetual source of convulsive surprises.

If we could only conceive an atom possessing consciousness then the whole world would turn into a Cosmic Computer, programmed every micro-second and giving answers at the same time. But, of course, the author should not be taken too seriously in this speculation as he is merely thinking aloud. Nonetheless, as Reichenbach suggested, there could be an accretion of Time-tagged marks on all matter.

Space is filled with cosmic bodies, dust and hydrogen. There is no empty space as such. In like manner, there cannot be any vacuums in Time. To say that the past is dead, the future not yet born, is to exist on a barrier between two non-existences. Scientifically and philosophically, this is not sound thinking.

If there is all-Time in which past, present and future co-exist in a qualitative relationship, then our lives have meaning and purpose. With deep insight into the essence of Time Shakespeare said:

There is a history in all men's lives,
Figuring the nature of the times deceased,
The which observed, a man may prophesy,
With a near aim, of the main chance of things
As yet not come to life, which in their seeds
And weak beginnings lie intreasured.
*Such things become the hatch and brood of Time.**

It is not within the scope of this work to determine *how* men have been able to prophesy. For a working hypothesis let us assume that the past and future are no less real than the present, that they are merely stages in changes taking place in the universe BEFORE and AFTER a certain arbitrary point called NOW. In this case it is possible to see past events or even glimpse future possibilities. This conclusion is of paramount importance to inventors of Time Machines.

This view will be illustrated by testimonies of those who have watched past happenings, generations after they have taken place, and the Time Travellers who have gazed at the panorama of the future.

An appearance of a past scene to one or several observers can be termed a *Time Reverberation*. These phenomena are usually connected with a certain place as if the place itself carries a memory of past events.

Because *Time Reverberation* reports could not be explained, they have often been discarded or classed as ghost stories and illusions.

On a wet October evening in 1916 Edith Olivier walked near Avebury and suddenly encountered a succession of huge grey megaliths on either hand. In the distance she saw a village fair. There is nothing unusual in seeing giant stones in a place like Avebury. A village fair is not uncommon in England, either. However, the megalithic alley

Henry IV, II, III, 1.

which Miss Olivier saw, had disappeared before 1800. The last fair in the district took place in 1853. Edith Olivier was not aware of this as she strolled in the green fields of Avebury in 1916.*

During World War I the battle of Mons took place on the same ground as a 15th-century combat between the English archers and the French army. Under a strong German attack the British were about to retreat when they saw their armoured ancestors with arbalests marching towards the German lines. The British soldiers followed the phantom troops and stopped the attack. If this was an hallucination, what had started it? Why were the warriors dressed in the attire of the 15th century? Was this merely a Time picture of the battle of that century?

The story of the Phantom Cavalcade of Rodenstein is supported by a number of written statements made in the 18th century. The barons of the castles of Rodenstein and Schnellert in Germany were ruthless bandits who terrorised the countryside by their crimes. In their escapades from one castle to the other, they robbed and kidnapped innocent people. The reports say that in the course of centuries numerous witnesses heard the passage of an invisible cavalcade on a road which had long since disappeared. The sound of carriage wheels, horses' feet, smacking of whips, blowing of horns, barking of dogs, and the voices of the desperadoes echoed between Rodenstein and Schnellert.†

Time reverberations can be visual as in the case of Edith Olivier, or audible as in the phenomenon of the Phantom Cavalcade. They represent episodes in breaking the Time barrier and seeing or hearing the past as real life. There are well-authenticated incidents in which persons involuntarily or voluntarily explored the future.

*E. Olivier, *Without Knowing Mr. Walkley*, London, 1939.
†C. Crow, *The Night Side of Nature*, London, 1848.

The *Evening News* (London) published a remarkable story on January 18, 1935. It came from an Englishman, H. Richards, who lived at 11 Rue Vauquelin, Dieppe, France. On October 9, 1934, King Alexander of Yugoslavia and the French Foreign Minister Jean Louis Barthou were assassinated in Marseilles. Mr. Richards saw it all in a precognitive dream, and realising the possible danger to the two statesmen who defied Hitler, decided to report his experiences to the authorities in Paris.

"Arriving in Paris the night before the assassination in Marseilles last October, I occupied—though this was unknown to me then—the room in a hotel that one of the terrorist conspirators had been given before leaving for Marseilles. Between 2 and 3 a.m. I had a vivid dream, the scene of which was a strange street in a strange town. The feature of it was the shooting of two men, one of whom I recognised as M. Barthou (from having seen him often), and the other I identified from next morning's papers as King Alexander. I repeated my dream to a friend, a Corsican, who is one of the chiefs of the Sûreté Nationale.

"Never sceptical of the occult, this official was so much impressed, especially when he recognised the section of the Canebière at Marseilles from my description of the street I had seen, that he telephoned at once to a colleague at Marseilles to record the incident. He was laughed at for his pains until the afternoon brought tragedy. It was this message that gave rise to the widely spread rumour that the police in Paris had warned Marseilles of the plot in good time."

Dr. Alexis Carrel, Nobel Prize winner, admits that projection into Time is a reality: "There is in certain individuals a psychical element capable of travelling in Time. They seem to wander as easily in Time as in space."*

*A. Carrel, *Man the Unknown*, New York, 1935.

Professor Nicholas Roerich, the famous explorer and artist, who lived in the Himalayas for many years, told an interesting episode that happened to him personally which illustrates the theory that man is able to have glimpses of the future:

"A lama came from Tibet shortly before our departure. We asked him if he had had visions or extraordinary dreams. This he denied at first: 'No, nothing of that sort ever happens. I am an ordinary lama.' A true lama would never divulge his faculties until his confidence was gained. We said to him: 'Let us know if you do experience something.'

"The next morning the visitor came back and in a perfectly calm, simple voice declared: 'I have seen'. And then in the same perfectly quiet manner he described our coming journey about which no local inhabitant in the Himalayas could have known. The itinerary he mapped out verbally did not, of course, indicate names but only descriptions. However, these descriptions were surprising in their accuracy and specific details. There were the sea voyage and stay in Paris, then a storm on the great sea, and America with its characteristic street traffic, city lights and skyscrapers. After that came the sea again, snow, a land with many temples and tame animals. Thereupon followed definite hints at the hills of Hingan in Manchuria. After that followed a description of another country with temples and large images of Buddha, and a distant land with tents, numerous sheep and horses.

"The epic was narrated in a quiet simple style as if the pilgrim was relating his own journey. The results of our voyage were also mentioned—something no one could have imagined beforehand. It seemed as if someone came up to the window and began to describe what was happening outside in the street."*

*N. Roerich, *Gates to the Future*, Riga, Latvia, 1936 (Russian).

The round-the-world voyage mentioned by Roerich covered India, France, U.S.A., the Pacific, Japan, Manchuria and Mongolia.

Is projection into the future or the past a chimerical idea? A person who is convinced that Time points towards the future only, may have a few surprises if he studies the properties of atomic particles. The positron is an electron travelling into the past!* He will also have a shock when he finds out that Time reversal in the nuclear world is a recognised fact.

16. SHIPS DRIFTING IN TIME

A PAST HAPPENING can re-appear today if we accept the concept of unified Time with past-present-future as one. But because of the overlapping of the past over the present in the same locale, the image would seem strange—like a double exposure in photography. Hence, the past scene on the background of the present would be interpreted as a mirage, an hallucination or illusion.

Its true definition is *Time Reverberation* or a perfectly realistic picture of actual people and objects from the past, unfolding before our eyes in the present.

Before going any further, let us agree on certain terms. A mirage is an atmospheric phenomenon due to light refraction, caused by sandwiched hot and cold air. A distant oasis with a spring mirrored in the heated air is seen in the arid Sahara. Mirages take place in the crystal-clear cold air of Antarctica as well. Cars driven hundreds of kilometres away show up on the Antarctic horizon. On fine days Fata Morgana is not an uncommon sight in the

*According to Dr. R. Feinman, Nobel Prize Laureate.

Straits of Messina, Toyama Bay and the Great Lakes. Due to lack of light and the absence of refraction, mirages do not occur at night. Neither are they seen in cloudy weather, fog or storm. An illusion is a misinterpretation—that is, a certain thing is taken for something else. But an hallucination is a psychological impression without any outside stimulus, usually caused by emotion, excitement, fear, drugs, alcohol or delusions due to an unbalanced mind. An apparition is a perception of unreal objects or persons, generally explained either as an illusion or an hallucination. A ghost is an alleged appearance of the dead to the living.

Ships with masts, rigging and sails have neither soul nor afterlife. They are solid vessels made of timber, iron and canvas built to sail the seven seas. This chapter is about "spectre ships" which drift out of the past.

The *Flying Dutchman* was believed to cruise around the Cape of Good Hope for centuries. The legend has it that in the second half of the 17th century Captain Vanderdecken swore a profane oath that he would round the Cape during a heavy storm though he should beat against the wind till Doomsday.

After examining numerous seamen's reports Captain Frederick Marryat of the Royal Navy (1792-1848) wrote *The Phantom Ship* in 1839. Sightings of this ship at night or in stormy weather cannot be explained as mirages. Captain Marryat tells the tale of the Dutch captain's son—Philip Vanderdecken—and how he and other sailors saw his father's phantom ship:

"At sunset the captain, Hillebrant and Philip directed their eyes to the quarter pointed out and thought they could perceive something like a vessel. Gradually the gloom seemed to clear away, and a lambent pale blaze to light up that part of the horizon.

"Not a breath of wind was on the water—the sea was like a mirror—more and more distinct did the vessel appear, till her hull, masts and yards were clearly visible. In the centre of the pale light, which extended about fifteen degrees above the horizon, there was indeed a large ship about three miles distant. But although it was a perfect calm, she was to all appearance buffeting in a violent gale, plunging and lifting over a surface that was smooth as glass, now careering to her bearing, then recovering herself.

"She made little way through the water but apparently neared them fast, driven down by the force of the gale. Each minute she was plainer to the view. At last, she was seen to wear and in so doing, before she was brought to the wind on the other tack, she was so close to them that they could distinguish the men on board.

"They could see the foaming water as it was hurled from her bows, hear the shrill whistle of the boatswain's pipes, the creaking of the ship's timbers, and the complaining of her masts. And then the gloom gradually rose, and in a few seconds she had totally disappeared.

"He turned round and met the one eye of Schriften, who screamed in his ear: 'Philip Vanderdecken, that's the *Flying Dutchman*!'"

Then the English captain describes the spectre ship, observed from another boat under entirely different weather conditions:

"It was a large ship on a wind and on the same tack as they were. In a gale, in which no vessel could carry the topsails, the *Vrow Katerina*, being under close-reefed foresails and staysails, the ship seen to leeward was standing under a press of sail—top gallant-sail, royals, flying jib, and every stitch of canvas which could be set in a light breeze.

"The waves were running mountains high, bearing each minute the *Vrow Katerina* down to the gunwale, and the ship seen appeared not to be affected by the tumultuous waters, but sailed steadily and smoothly on an even keel."

Captain Marryat then tells how the captain of the *Batavia* with twenty men and a priest encountered the *Flying Dutchman* in the dark of night:

"The night was fine and the heavens clear. I had turned in when about two o'clock in the morning the mate called me to come on deck. No banks up to windward, and yet a fog in the middle of a clear sky, with a fresh breeze, and with water all around it. For, you see, the fog did not cover more than half a dozen cables' length, as we could perceive by the horizon on each side of it. Then I heard voices. And then we heard the bell toll.

"'It must be a vessel,' I said to the mate. 'Not of this world, sir!' he replied. And then the fog and all disappeared as if by magic."

In the *Phantom Ship* the English naval officer quotes another equally fantastic account:

"A bank of clouds rose up from the eastward, with a rapidity that, to the seamen's eyes, was unnatural, and it soon covered the whole firmament. The sun was obscured and all was one deep and unnatural gloom. The wind subsided and the ocean was hushed. In the cabin the increased darkness was first observed by Philip, who went on deck. He was followed by the captain and passengers who were in a state of amazement.

"'There! There!' shouted the sailors, pointing to the beam of the vessel. On the beam of the ship, not more than two cables' length distant, they beheld, slowly rising out of the water, the tapering masthead and spars of another vessel. She rose, and rose gradually, her topmasts and topsails yards, with the sails set, next made their appearance—higher and higher she rose up from the element. Her lower masts and rigging, and lastly, her hull showed itself above the surface. Still she rose up till her ports, with her guns, and at last the whole of her floatage was above water.

" 'Holy Virgin!' exclaimed the captain, breathless. 'I have known ships to go down but never to come up before!' "

Weather conditions unsuitable for a mirage, the presence of a localised mist, a feeling of gloom and a sudden vanishing—are the common features of these *Flying Dutchman* sightings. It is odd indeed that voices and bells had been heard in these phenomena which proves they were not mirages.

Captain Marryat says to the *Flying Dutchman*: "Time has stopped with you but with those who live in the world it stops not." A Time dilation is undoubtedly at work in the occurrences of spectre ships. It is interesting to note that the phantom ships usually carry tragedies with them, as if violent passions left strong imprints on space creating a force field on a subatomic level.

These phantoms come out of eternity, re-enacting the past—they are Time clichés with movement and sequence, mirror-images of yesterday.

A French motion picture team in Morocco observed in 1928 a spectacle in the sky which was more exciting than some of the films they had taken. Overhead they saw a fleet with sails and pennants travelling from the Atlantic inland into the Sahara. The vast armada slowly drifted across the sky to vanish in the haze over the desert.*

The ships looked ancient—they had sails and bore strange pennants on their masts. The cameramen made notes of the pennant colours and markings, and the shape of the vessels.

When historical sources were consulted later, an amazing fact emerged. The craft were the kind that Spain and Portugal used for ocean voyages in the 14th century! According to Portuguese and Spanish archives, the flags belonged to the navies of Spain and Portugal but one vessel was Turkish.

*I. T. Sanderson, *Uninvited Visitors*, New York, 1967.

A further enquiry demonstrated that only once did the joint fleets of Spain and Portugal escort a Turkish ship in the Atlantic—and that was in the 14th century.

Mirages are images of objects refracted in the atmosphere now. They do not show up on the horizon six hundred years later.

Spectre ships are out of place in this age of spaceships. Yet if phantom ships were real in the past, there is no reason why the phenomenon should not be repeated today. In fact, these Time reverberations do occur nowadays.

For many generations a phantom ship has been seen between Cape Breton in Nova Scotia and Chaleur Bay in New Brunswick. The ship suddenly becomes visible on the surface of the sea. Sometimes it seems to be afire or surrounded with a glow.

The mystery boat does not have a set place or time to make its appearance. It has not been sighted for the past twenty years.

R. H. Sherwood, a writer in Nova Scotia, says in a letter: "I myself have seen it on three different occasions with possibly twenty years intervening. No one has ever taken a picture of it, and no one has ever caught up with it, although attempts have been made many times. It just disappears before their eyes." Many other residents of Nova Scotia and New Brunswick have watched the spectre ship, singly and in groups.

It has to be admitted that Time reverberations seldom happen. But one should not remove them from the field of scientific study just because they are rare.

Time reverberations can lead to the discovery of how past events are recorded in space. Then the next step would be to devise an electronic technique for showing pictures of the past on the Time Television screen.

In studying these echoes from the past it is logical to conclude that they are not caused by light or sound waves which have no source of emission at the time. But perhaps there are sub-atomic levels where everything that happened is somehow stored. This possibility has been suggested by Professor H. Reichenbach and Arthur Clarke, while the experiments of Professor Rémy Chauvin have demonstrated that atomic processes are influenced by human thought.

Also we cannot rule out the possible reflection of the scenes of today in the sea of cosmic matter. They may be reflected like radio waves, bouncing from the Appleton or Heaviside-Kennelly layers or travelling in space like televised lunar landscapes broadcast from the moon by our astronauts. Undoubtedly, we are here moving in an hypothetical and obscure region and can only speculate.

17. THE PETIT TRIANON MYSTERY

Two English ladies—Annie Moberley in her fifties and Eleanor Jourdain approaching forty—visited Paris in August 1901. They wrote one of the most impossible stories of the century.*

Who were they? Miss Annie Moberley was Principal of St. Hugh's Women's College at Oxford. Her father, Rev. George Moberley, Oxford don and Bishop of Salisbury, was born in Russia, claiming descent from Czar Peter the Great. Miss Moberley held an honorary degree of Master of Arts, Oxford.

Eleanor Frances Jourdain descended from a Huguenot family which had come to England from France. She was the daughter of Rev. Francis Jourdain, Vicar of Ash-bourne, Derbyshire. In 1903 Eleanor Jourdain was

*Moberley/Jourdain, *An Adventure*, London, 1948.

awarded a doctorate by the University of Paris. She studied Modern History at Oxford and was author of several books published by London editors. Among her colleagues and students Miss Jourdain had the reputation of being an accomplished musician.

After a brief stay in Paris the two Oxford teachers decided to see Versailles. They saw the palace and then came down by the great flight of stairs towards the canal. Then they walked through the park towards the Trianon.

At the Petit Trianon the Misses Moberley and Jourdain turned into a lane on their right. A plough lay in front of deserted farm buildings. Two men in long green coats and three-cornered hats stood on the path. Miss Jourdain asked them the way. In a grave manner the men made some gestures which the women understood as a direction to walk straight on. The English tourists kept on talking as they strolled. The strange costumes of the two men did not surprise them, at first.

A woman and a thirteen- or fourteen-year-old girl were standing at the doorway of a detached cottage. They wore white kerchiefs tucked into their bodices. According to Miss Jourdain: "The woman was standing on the steps, bending slightly forward, holding a jug in her hand. The girl was looking up at her from below with her hands raised, but nothing in them. She might have been just going to take the jug or have just given it up. I remember that both seemed to pause for an instant, as in a motion picture."

Soon an enclosed wood was in front of them. Within it stood a circular kiosk. The place looked eerie and forsaken and a feeling of depression came over the two English ladies. A man in a cloak and sombrero sat by the kiosk. His face, marked by smallpox, was repulsive. "I did not feel that he was looking particularly at us," wrote Miss Jourdain.

Suddenly a young-looking man in a dark coat and

buckled shoes came running and shouting excitedly something about "il ne faut pas passer par là". He then made a gesture to their right, saying, "par içi . . . cherchez la maison." The young man "said a great deal more than we could understand," wrote the French-speaking ladies from Oxford. Bowing with a curious smile the man vanished yet the sound of his footsteps could be heard for some time.

Silently the two companions passed over a small rustic bridge which crossed a ravine. A cascade fell down a green bank with ferns and stones. Beyond the bridge the path skirted a meadow surrounded by trees. A small country house with shuttered windows and terraces on both sides stood in the distance.

With her back to the house a lady was sitting on the lawn. She held a large sheet of paper or cardboard in her hands and appeared to be sketching or looking at it. The lady was not too young, but attractive. She wore an unusual summer dress arranged on her shoulders in kerchief fashion. It was long-waisted with a good deal of fullness in the skirt which seemed to be short. A shady white hat covered her fair hair. As they turned in their walk Miss Moberley noticed that the lady's fichu was pale green.

There seemed to be a second house at the continuation of the terrace and the English visitors approached it. Suddenly a door flung open and then closed with a bang as a young man with the manner of a footman but no livery came out. The ladies received the impression that they were trespassing and followed him towards the Petit Trianon. All of a sudden, they found themselves among a crowd dressed in 1901 fashion, obviously attending a wedding party. From the Versailles Palace the tourists took a carriage to the Hôtel des Réservoirs.

Back in England, the two co-workers reviewed their experiences at the Petit Trianon and found them odd. In the course of a conversation on November 10, 1901 they discovered that Miss Jourdain had not seen the lady with the sheet of paper sitting in the meadow. On the other hand, Miss Moberley had not noticed the plough nor the woman and the girl with a jug. This did not make sense. Then they analysed the theatrical costumes of the people they met at the Petit Trianon and the unaccountable feeling of weirdness which came over them that afternoon on August 10, 1901. Moberley and Jourdain decided to compare notes and gather all possible information about the Petit Trianon in order to find an explanation.

In July 1904 the two Oxford pedagogues revisited the Petit Trianon. They discovered that the cottage, in front of which Miss Jourdain had seen a woman with a girl, was completely changed. The spot where they had met the two men in the 18th-century coats and hats, looked different. They tried to locate the old paths but without success— somehow "the distances were contracted" as they said in their book *An Adventure*.

The kiosk had vanished and so had the cascade and the little bridge. A bush grew on the meadow where the lady had been sitting. The house with the terrace had also changed its appearance.

This was a challenge to the two Oxford women and they began a systematic research which took several years. They bought old maps of Versailles, consulted documents at the Bibliothèque Nationale and corresponded with historians. One by one, the riddles were analysed and often solved.

The plough Miss Jourdain saw was undoubtedly out of place at the Petit Trianon palace. However, it was established that an old plough had been kept at the Petit Trianon and subsequently sold after the Revolution.

Green uniforms were worn only by Royal servants at Versailles. The two men in green coats and three-cornered hats were identified as the brothers Bersy who were on guard on the last day of Queen Marie-Antoinette's stay at the Petit Trianon on October 5, 1789.

From a map they discovered that the cottage had once stood near the entrance. A plan of Versailles made about 1783 disclosed that there had been a round pavilion with pillars about the time of the French Revolution. It was different from the Temple de l'Amour which is still in existence.

The Album Modène (in Biblioteca Estense in Modena, Italy) corroborated the layout of the grounds in 1789 as seen by Moberley and Jourdain.

From Lavergne's *Légendes de Trianon* the girl's name was found to be Marion and she was fourteen years old in 1789. Historical research led to the identity of the dark man in a sombrero. He was the Count de Vaudreuil, a pock-marked Creole who played a part in bringing about Marie-Antoinette's downfall. In 1789 the sombrero was becoming fashionable.

The running man who seemed to come "either over, round or through a rock" was thought to have been the page de Bretagne. He was dispatched by the Minister of the Palace to the Trianon with an urgent warning to the Queen to leave immediately as the revolutionaries were on the way from Paris.

In 1902 Miss Moberley saw Wertmüller's portrait of Marie-Antoinette and was struck by its resemblance to the lady on the lawn. Archives revealed that the Queen's modiste Madame Eloffe did make two green silk bodices in the summer of 1789.

The door from which a footman appeared had been blocked since the French Revolution. His name was thought to have been Lagrange, and his duties as porter comprised the keeping away of strangers.

From historical sources the English teachers realised that the Queen had been in the gardens at the time she received the warning on October 5, 1789. The messenger insisted that the Queen go to 'la Maison' (the Petit Trianon) to get ready for escape. Then he ran in an excited state for a carriage.

Annie Moberley and Eleanor Jourdain theorised that as Marie-Antoinette was going through mental torture in the Hall of Assembly on August 10, 1792, she cast her mind back to her last day at the Petit Trianon on October 5, 1789. The Oxford women thought that they "had inadvertently entered within an act of the Queen's memory when alive," exactly one hundred and nine years later—on August 10, 1901.

The findings and interpretations of the teachers of St. Hugh's can be rejected and the experience explained in terms of an illusion, unless this was a case of a Time reverberation.

To see 18th-century buildings and landscape about the character of which only the experts had known excludes auto-suggestion. The hallucination hypothesis is not strong—the experiences in the gardens of the Petit Trianon took almost half-an-hour with two individuals participating in them.

There were several contradictions in the reports which seemed as baffling to the English pedagogues as they are to us. Only Miss Moberley saw the lady on the lawn whom she took for a tourist. Miss Jourdain alone noticed the woman with the girl, moving one instant and frozen the next. She observed the plough in front of an empty-looking building. Miss Moberley saw the building but not the plough. These incongruities were never denied by the women.

At the time of the experience they assumed that whatever one saw, the other did as well. It was only at Oxford that they realised that many things were odd in their visit to Versailles.

If the two English tourists were objectively watching a re-enactment of happenings on October 5, 1789, from the afternoon of August 10, 1901, how can we explain their alleged conversations with people from another point in Time? The critical question is—were the two guards, the running man and the porter talking with the English women? Let us suppose that three people are standing more or less one behind the other. The person in front may wave to the person farthest away, while the one between them will assume that the signal is for him.

This explains why the directions given by the two uniformed men were not satisfactory to the English ladies. "They answered in a seemingly casual and mechanical way," wrote Moberley and Jourdain. Actually, the instructions were not correct at all—"we came out sufficiently near the first lane we had been in, to make me wonder why the garden officials had not directed us back instead of telling us to go forward," they wrote in *An Adventure*. The answer is this—the officials were not talking to them, 20th-century beings.

The man on the path in an excited state appeared out of nowhere like Mephistopheles in *Faust*. He was shouting "long unintelligible sentences," mentioning "la maison." It was not because Miss Jourdain could not understand the language but because nothing that was shouted made any sense to her except "not to pass that way and look for la maison". This was Marie-Antoinette's name for the Petit Trianon. The messenger was not addressing the English tourists in the 20th century but shouting to the Queen or someone else about the urgent message to leave Versailles after packing in "la maison".

The young man made his exit in a queer manner—he vanished while his running footsteps could still be heard for a while after his disappearance.

The servant who slammed the door with a bang, yet spoke in whispers, did not lead them out. The English ladies merely followed him.

Julie Lavergne in *Légendes de Trianon* describes the events of October 5, 1789. Marie-Antoinette had been walking and talking to Marion, the gardner's daughter, before coming to her favourite spot in the gardens She sat in the meadow and some time later called Marion. Instead of the girl, a "garçon de la chambre" appeared in an excited frame of mind. He brought a letter warning the Queen of the approach of the mobs from Paris, due in an hour. There was not much time to spare. The messenger bowed and ran to order a carriage while Marie-Antoinette followed him to "la maison"—the Petit Trianon. This was the Queen's last day at Versailles. The source of this story is Marion herself.

It is a notable fact that on August 10, 1901, electric storms swept over Europe. The static in the atmosphere could have amplified the *temporal field*.

The British mathematician J. W. Dunne commented thus on this strange case: "Hence, if Einstein is right, the contents of Time are just as real as the contents of space. Marie-Antoinette, body and brain, is sitting in the Trianon now."

Were these two English women projected into an historic past? In a pre-Einsteinian epoch this question would have been ridiculed because science knew nothing of the relativity of Time.

Let us cross into the domain of science-fiction for a while. Before us is a paper tape with the letters of the alphabet from A to Z. The letter Z is the last moment in Time or NOW. It is obvious that by bending or folding the tape our Z, or the present instant, can touch any of the letters before it, or the past. Perhaps it is by this Hyper-Time that the projection into the past is accomplished.

Except for the final scene—the wedding, the people and some of the buildings, the Oxford teachers saw—everything belonged to the 18th century. But neither the persons nor the landscapes were stable—as if 18th-century life was superimposed on 20th-century scenery for certain periods of time.

It is reasonable to think that the Petit Trianon mystery is a Time reverberation. Certain peculiarities of the phenomena observed by the English women link them with the distinguishing marks of a radio or television programme—fading of sounds, melting of images, wavering of scenes and so on.

Passages from the book *An Adventure* will prove these conclusions. This is what Miss Moberley writes about the sudden appearance of a landscape from another century: "Everything suddenly looked unnatural, therefore unpleasant; even the trees behind the building seemed to have become flat and lifeless, like a wood worked in tapestry. There were no effects of light and shade, and no wind stirred the trees. It was all intensely still." Miss Jourdain confirmed this impression in these words: "The whole scene—sky, trees and buildings gave a little shiver, like the movement of a curtain or of scenery as at a theatre." Had she lived to the great age of television, she would have compared it to wavering images on a TV screen.

One of the strangest manifestations at the Petit Trianon was the episode of the woman and the girl, who was handing her a jug. All of a sudden there was a pause in the action as if a motion picture stopped and became a "still". For some reason the flow of events was interrupted for an instant. This change in Time rate was known to the ancients as we can glean from the Apocryphal New Testament:

"And behold there were sheep being driven, and they went not forward but stood still; and the shepherd lifted his hand to smite them with his staff, and his hand remained up. And all of a sudden, all things moved onward on their course."*

*M. R. James, *The Apocryphal New Testament*, Oxford, 1926.

The events of the 18th and 20th centuries co-exist in space. Miss Jourdain clearly points to the existence of a "force field": "I felt as though I was being taken up into another condition of things quite as real as the former." This is a confirmation of the relativist viewpoint that objects separated by Time can occupy the same space.

Intuitively the Misses Moberley and Jourdain understood that theirs was an experience which some day might be of great value to science. This is what C. A. E. Moberley wrote in a letter: "We have felt we were trustees for something bigger than could be at present understood and that we must bravely make it public and put up with the inevitable incredulity which would follow."

Landale Johnson in *The Trianon Case* writes of an American, his wife and son who also saw a lady in white and a man in a three-cornered hat at the Trianon. The figures came into sight out of nowhere and disappeared in the same way. The incidents took place early in this century, and their written statement is in the Bodleian Library at Oxford. In 1914 the Americans met Misses Moberley and Jourdain to share their experiences.

Another confirmation came from Miss C. M. Burrow and her companion who saw an old man in the green and silver livery and the three-cornered hat of pre-Revolution days. The episode occurred in October 1928 and they had not read Moberley and Jourdain's book.

18. FROM YESTERDAY TO TOMORROW

THE PETIT TRIANON story and other cases of Time reverberation open wide horizons of regions unexplored and might facilitate the invention of Time Television.

The conclusion that the past is gone forever is only

partially true. Past happenings do exist somewhere on the temporal axis. To doubt the reality of the past is to undermine the reality of the present which is built upon it.

Apparently, we lean too much on the evidence of the five senses. To depend upon physical perceptions without making corrections is to believe the seeming movement of the sun around the Earth, the flatness of the Earth and the small size of the stars.

If past, present and future constitute one reality, then somewhere far away in Time Mark Antony falls on a sword to kill himself, Cleopatra picks up a poisonous snake to join him in the hereafter, Jesus delivers the Sermon on the Mount, Galileo argues with the Inquisition and Napoleon commands the Grand Armée at Austerlitz. These are fixed historical landmarks which are quite concrete. When we deal with the future, a sea of probability stretches before us. How can we conceive of something which has not taken place or may not occur at all?

Today is yesterday's tomorrow. Tomorrow will soon become today. Today is but a reference point from which we count Time distances and orient ourselves.

In infinity there is no absolute UP or DOWN. Neither does eternity have any BEFORE or AFTER. The past makes the present. The present creates the future. Sir Oliver Lodge once said in an address: "The events may be in some sense in existence always, both past and future, and it may be we who are arriving at them, not they which are happening." This is a relativist interpretation of the scope of Time.

It is indeed startling to imagine that the gallery of past history is like Madame Tussaud's wax museum. How much more remarkable is the possibility that the contours of the future have already been marked by the actions of yesterday and today? Every action produces a result for there are no effectless causes or causeless effects.

In his book *An Experiment with Time* J. W. Dunne writes that if the mentally imposed barrier which ties us to the present is removed—it is possible to have glimpses of the future.

In the *Natural Philosophy of Time* G. J. Withrow propounds the idea that Time may be essentially a macroscopic phenomenon. He thinks that the evidence for precognition could perhaps be explained in terms of transcending this macroscopic Time. In his opinion, on the subatomic scale there may be no direction of Time—forwards or backwards.

This hypothesis may, perhaps, explain how seers move on the Time axis and gain advance knowledge of events which have not yet happened.

It will be shown in the following chapters that prophets have been able to see the future. And although these visions are sometimes recorded in symbols and allegories, their veracity is nevertheless astonishing.

19. HISTORY IN A PACK OF CARDS

IN HIS NINE-VOLUME WORK *Le Monde Primitif* (1773-1783) Antoine Court de Gébelin of the Royal Academy of La Rochelle alluded to an ancient Egyptian book which had escaped the fire of the Alexandrian Library during Julius Caesar's invasion of Egypt.

"It contained their teaching in an uncorrupt state on subjects of the most interesting nature. This book of ancient Egypt is the game of Tarots—we have it in cards," he wrote two hundred years ago.

Far-fetched speculation? Possibly, yet the Oriental source

of the Tarot cards is substantiated by the presence of a sphinx on the tenth card *The Wheel of Fortune* and also by the name of the second card *La Papessa*—a blasphemous title in the Catholic countries of Italy, Spain and France, where the cards made their debut. The name of the card points to a connection with the East where the High Priestess was in antiquity a part of the state cult.

The initial 78 playing cards comprised 22 *Tarocchi* and 56 cards marked with figures and pips in the four suits. In the course of centuries the 22 Tarots as well as the 4 *Knight* cards were dropped from the pack, leaving the 52 cards in our modern set of playing cards.

The original 78 playing cards were employed exclusively for recreation and gambling. Fortune-telling by cards came a century or two after the Tarot's appearance about 1325. The gipsies did not bring the Tarot from Asia. They first came to Paris in August 1427 when the cards had already been in circulation for a century.

The earliest 14th-century cards were called *Naibi* in Italy and *Naypes* in Spain. These non-Latin names were derived from the Arabic *Nabi*, or a prophet. The Tarot thus presents a paradox—the card *La Papessa* was an affront to the Church in Christendom while the Arabic name of the cards *Nabi* was profanity in the lands of Islam where the word *Prophet* was not said in vain. Furthermore, the Koran forbade gambling and the Arabs did not play cards. The subject of the origin of the Tarot is not only a paradox but a riddle.

The solution may be found in an hypothesis that the Templars received these symbolic tablets from a secret fraternity, such as the Druses of Lebanon, at the Order's fortress at Acre. The path of the Tarot may have begun at the Pyramids leading to Baalbek, Acre and eventually Paris, the seat of the Order of the Temple.

About the year 1300 dark clouds gathered over the

Templars. Their citadel at Acre was captured by the Sultan of Syria in 1291. On "Black Friday", October 13, 1307, the Order of the Temple was crushed by the King of France and the Pope of Rome.

The date of the appearance of the Tarot strangely coincides with the time of the disbandment of the Order. The Templars could have decided to release their symbolic cards shortly before the persecution. The Tarot, pronounced TARO in French, may be an anagram for ORTA, or the *Or*der of *Te*mple (pronounced *Ta*mple in French).

Similarly Albert Pike 33° Mason discovered one hundred years ago, the initials of the last Grand Master of the Templars—Jacques Bertrand de Molay—had been concealed in the passwords of the three major Masonic degrees.

The book *Gulden Spiel* published by Günther Zainer in Augsburg in 1472, indicates that playing cards were introduced into Germany about 1300 A.D.

Alphonso XI, King of Castile, founded the Order of La Banda in 1332. Its statutes prohibited the knights "to play at cards or dice."

In his *Histoire et Chronique de Provence* (Lyons, 1614) César Nostradamus writes that playing cards were recorded in the Chronicle of Provence in the year 1361. These early entries are casual, implying that the cards were fairly well known at the time.

There are no documents previous to 1300 mentioning the existence of the 78 playing cards. However, the evidence of an indirect nature, such as the symbology of the cards themselves, makes this conjecture plausible.

The antiquity of the Tarots was accepted as fact by Christian Pitois (P. Christian), the Librarian of the Ministry of Education in the reign of Napoleon III. In his *Histoire de la Magie* he refers to Iamblichus and paints a scene of initiation in ancient Egypt:

"The initiate sees a long gallery supported by caryatides in the form of twenty-four sphinxes, twelve on each side. On each part of the wall between two sphinxes there are fresco paintings, representing figures and mysterious symbols. These twenty-two pictures face one another in pairs.

"A time followed when Egypt, no longer able to struggle against her invaders, prepared to die honourably. Then the Egyptian savants (at least so my mysterious informant asserts) held a great assembly to arrange how knowledge, which until that date had been confined to men judged worthy to receive it, should be saved from destruction."

Christian Pitois then relates how the "most important scientific secrets" were engraved on small plates—the Tarot. It is not improbable that until the 14th century the secret brotherhoods of Egypt, Syria and Palestine, as well as the Order of the Temple, were the custodians of the symbolic Tarot tablets. After the brutal massacre of the Knights Templar, the surviving members of the Order gave the pack to gamblers in the conviction that vice would preserve the ancient cryptogram for generations to come. This confidence has been fully justified.

Indisputably, this story is not history. However, it can be taken as a working theory. The writings of Court de Gébelin and Christian Pitois intimate that the Tarot plates were created some time before the Roman occupation of Egypt in 47 B.C.

The year 100 B.C. opened the zodiacal cycle of Pisces. In the precession of the equinoxes the sun retrogrades through the twelve signs of the zodiac at the rate of about 2,200 years in each sign. That year was a logical time for the wise priests of the Land of the Pyramids to leave a message for future ages, particularly in view of the anticipated end of Egypt's 5,000-year-old culture.

Does the name *Nabi* (a prophet) reveal the prophetic

purpose of the cards? The key to the enigma of the Tarot is probably concealed in the last card *Il Mondo*, or the Universe, which displays the cardinal signs of the zodiac —Aquarius, Scorpio, Leo and Taurus in the four corners of the card in the form of an angel, eagle, lion and bull, known to ancient Egyptians.

Firstly, this card establishes an historical connection with Egypt. The sphinx was depicted on ancient frescoes with a human face, body of a bull, legs of a lion, and wings of an eagle* which correspond with the four zodiacal signs of the *Il Mondo* card. Secondly, this "cosmic" card with the zodiacal signs and the image of Isis or Nature, the Universal Mother, proclaims the astronomical and astrological significance of the Tarot. In using the word "astrological" we do not uphold the superstition that the stars rule our lives. But the sun, moon, planets and stars are sources of radiation which exercise influence upon the earth.

The Soviet astronomer P. R. Romanchuck found a connection between sun spots and the positions of the planets, particularly in squares and conjunctions.

In the Russian magazine *Znanie-Sila* (No. 12, 1967), A. Gangnus writes: "In ancient times astrologers attempted to predict the future by the respective positions of the planets. Who knows, this may not be so absurd. If the respective positions of the planets really influence the sun, then astronomical tables could become data for helio-geophysical and even long-range climatic forecasts."

The American scientist Wm. F. Corliss has recently stated that: "Stranger still is the observation that sunspot maxima are roughly synchronised with the French and Russian revolutions, both world wars, and the Korean

*Shown on the tunic of Tutenkhamun and a plaque of Ameno-phis III. Tradition says that the Sphinx of Giza was also decorated with wings on special occasions.

98

conflict. If there is some small truth in astrology, the thing to do is to explain this truth in scientific terms and strip away all the pretence."*

What astrology was yesterday, astronomy and astrophysics are today. In *Cognition of Distance and Time in Space* by the Soviet astronaut Leonov and V. I. Lebedev, it is said that there is a definite connection between explosions on the sun and happenings on our planet. "The number of car accidents increases four times on the second day after the solar flare-ups, as compared with the days when the sun is calm," they write. Puzzling is the shocking increase in suicides, also four or five times above the normal rate, during the periods of violent explosions on the sun.

These quotations from scientific sources should dispel some of the scepticism when one hears of the ancient tradition of astrological cycles.

According to the author's discovery, the twenty-two Tarot cards are prophecies for the twenty-two centuries of the Piscean age starting with the first century before our era. The Tarot is a calendar of history from 100 B.C. to about 2100 A.D. Each card of the Tarot pack portrays the events of a century in a symbolic message.

Examining the pageant of Time from the beginning of the first century before our era until our own times, amazing correspondences will be found between the symbols of the Tarot and historical events. The Tarot is a programme of world history which opened about 100 B.C. and will close in the latter part of the next century. There are twenty two acts in this universal drama, and Act 21 is now on the world's stage. It is difficult to say how the sages of ancient Egypt succeeded in breaking the Time Barrier. But break it they did.

The author has based his research on the Italian Tarot

*W. F. Corliss, *Mysteries of the Universe*, New York, 1967.

of the 14th century which, historically, is the oldest specimen.

IL BAGATTEL, or the Magician, stands in front of a table on which lie four symbolic articles—a cup, a coin, a rod and a sword. In the Magician one can recognise Osiris with "djed"—the tree trunk. The four objects on the table are the four "Children of Horus"—the cardinal points which accompany images of Osiris. Osiris was cruelly killed by Typhon. But he rose from the dead. In the Book of the Dead he says: "I am the resurrection." In the hymns to Osiris there are the words "I have not done evil to mankind. I am pure."

In this card one can discern the character of the first century before our era—the times of the Magi, the Ancient Mysteries, the Teacher of Righteousness of the Dead Sea Scrolls. Osiris was a water god. The first Christians, affiliated with the Essenes, used the sign of the fish, symbolic of the Piscean Age.

LA PAPESSA, or the High Priestess, the second card of the Tarot, depicts a stately woman with a tiara and a mantle, sitting on a throne. There is a cross on her chest and a book on her knees. This cards covers the first century of our era and is an allegory of the formation of the Christian Church. *La Papessa* is the Church with its tiara, cross and the Bible.

L'IMPERATRICE, or the Empress, is the name of the third card and it typifies events in the second century. A crowned woman with a sceptre, seated on a throne, holds a shield emblazoned with a hawk. This is a symbol of the grandeur of the Roman Empire in this propitious period. This is the age of Hadrian (76-138 A.D.), the Emperor-builder and Marcus Aurelius (121-180 A.D.), the philosopher-king. The cult of Isis rises to great heights—the Empress with the hawk is Isis with Horus, the Hawk.

L'IMPERATORE, or the Emperor, is the fourth card.

An emperor sitting on a throne holds a sceptre. There is a shield with an eagle by his side. The emperor's legs are crossed. This Tarot card stands for the third century. At the dawn of this period a decision is passed that a Roman Emperor be elected by the army. Emperor Diocletian (245-316 A.D.) makes attempts to stabilise the Roman Empire. The crossed legs of the Emperor may allude to Christianity. A reign of terror over the first Christians broke out in this century.

IL PAPA, or the Pope, is the fifth Tarot card. The Pope's right hand makes the sign of benediction and his left rests on a triple cross. Two ecclesiastics face the Pope. This tablet is a pictorial forecast for the fourth century. The name of the card, the triple cross and the bishop's tiara convey an ecclesiastical meaning. It is an accurate portrayal of the events in this century—the establishment of Christianity as the state religion by the Council of Nicea in 325 A.D. In 300 A.D. Christianity became the official cult of Britain.

GLI AMANTI, or the Lovers, also called the *Two Ways*, is the sixth Tarot card. A young man stands between two young women at a crossing. One of the women wears a diadem and a mantle, the other has a wreath of flowers and a light dress. No better picture could have been painted to depict allegorically the separation of Western and Eastern Roman Empires in the fifth century. The girl in the long robe is the West or Rome, the young woman with a garland in an exotic dress is the East or Byzantium.

IL CARRO, or the Chariot, is the seventh card which covers events in the sixth century. A warrior rides in a chariot drawn by two horses. He holds the rod of power in one hand, and a sword in the other. Two crescents are attached to the shoulders of the charioteer. The triumphant warrior is Mohammed born in 570 A.D. wearing crescents, the badges of Islam. This is also the glorious age of Emperor Justinian who codified Roman Law.

LA GIUSTIZIA, or Justice, is the name of the eighth Tarot. A woman in an iron crown carries a sword and scales. She symbolises the Law of Islam carried by the sword in the name of Justice. The card illustrates the rise of the Arab Empire in the seventh century.

L'ERMITA, or the Hermit, is the ninth card and it shows an old man with a lamp and a staff walking in the night. This Tarot covers the eighth century and it is a symbolic picture of Islam obscured by the battle of Poitiers-Tours in 732 A.D. The old man is the allegory of the decline of the Arab Empire.

RUOTA DELLA FORTUNA, or the Wheel of Fortune, is the tenth Tarot card containing a forecast for the ninth century. A monkey and a dog turn a wheel over which hovers a sphinx with a dart. The Wheel of Fortune turns with the crowning of Charlemagne in 800. The rule of the Divine Right of Kings is established to last for a thousand years. The system of feudalism becomes a permanent institution. The Carolingian Renaissance—the beginning of learning in the Occident—is portrayed by the Sphinx, the eternal symbol of wisdom.

LA FORZA, or the Force, is the eleventh tablet showing a woman with a long mantle and a wide-brimmed hat taming a defiant lion. This is the tenth century. The woman in the ecclesiastical costume is the Church. The lion is an emblem of royalty. This card symbolises the ascendancy of the papacy and the struggle between the Church and the State which characterise this century. In 962 Pope John XII crowns Otto of Germany but in 963 the Pope is deposed by the Emperor. This conflict between the Church and the Sovereign reaches its climax in the following century when Henry IV is humiliated at Canossa by Pope Gregory.

L'APESSO, or the Hanged Man, is the twelfth card. On the backdrop of a night sky with the half-moon rises a gallows. A man with bound hands is hanging by a leg. The other leg is bent, forming a cross. The Hanged Man covers the eleventh century in this ancient Book of Time. This century opens with the profanation of the Holy Sepulchre by the Mohammedans in 1009 and closes with the occupation of Jerusalem by the Crusaders in 1099. The crossed legs are again a reference to the trials of Christianity as represented on Card 4, the Emperor. The crescent is an obvious allusion to Islam. This is the century of victims, Christian and Mohammedan alike, killed by the sword and sickness.

LA MORTE, or Death, is the name of the thirteenth Tarot card containing a prophecy for the twelfth century. It shows a skeleton armed with a scythe mowing down human heads. The tablet augurs ill for the world. More crusades are fought and Jerusalem is retaken by Saladin (1138-1193). The Reaping Skeleton is an excellent representation of Genghis Khan (1162–1227), whose hordes emerge from Mongolia and reach the Adriatic, leaving pyramids of skulls behind.

LA TEMPERANZA, or Temperance, is the fourteenth card which bears a message for the thirteenth century. An angel with two urns is pouring a liquid from one vessel into the other. In this symbology, the old wine of classical culture is poured into the empty jug of medieval darkness. The splendid era of the Renaissance is born. New times come as Dante (1265-1321) writes his book *New Life* and introduces into Europe the classic ideal of happiness. Roger Bacon (1214-1294) criticises the scholastics and prepares the way for the age of science. This is the century of the Magna Carta (1215) when temperance in government is first introduced. The travels of Marco Polo (1254-1324) build a bridge between Asia and

Europe and contribute to an influx of new ideas—hence the allegory of the angel with the two urns.

IL DIAVOLO, or the Devil, is the fifteenth card. A horned monster with bat-like wings and a burning torch in his hand stands on a pedestal to which are chained two satyrs. This tablet portends evil for the fourteenth century. The Devil's torch starts the Hundred Years War between England and France in 1337. The black wings of Satan cover all of Europe with the dread Black Death, or plague (1347-1350).

LA TORRE, or the Tower, on the sixteenth Tarot card allegorises events in the fifteenth century. Lightning from the sun strikes the tower. A crowned man is falling from the top of the tower while a monk already lies on the ground. What does the card mean? The lightning from the sun is a symbol of the discovery of printing by Gutenberg (1400-1468) which spread the light of knowledge. But it undermined Church scholasticism and royal authority, hence the falling king and priest. As people of Europe began to read widely, they commenced to speculate. The privilege to think freely is fatal to dogma. Concepts are shaken like a stricken tower as Christopher Columbus discovers America in 1492. The Old World is indeed struck by lightning.

LE STELLE, or the Stars, is the seventeenth cryptogram. Brilliant stars shine in the sky. A naked young woman sits on the bank of a river. She has two vessels from which water pours down. A singing bird rests on a bush nearby. On this card is marked the tone of the sixteenth century. *The Stars* card represents the century of astronomers—Copernicus died in 1543, Tycho de Brahe was born in 1546, Giordano Bruno in 1548, Kepler in 1571 and Galileo in 1564. Again, as on Card 14, two vases appear—an allegory of new times. On that card they stood for the Renaissance and here the urns are a metaphor of the Reformation. Martin Luther (d. 1546) attempts to purify Christianity. Also this is the Elizabethan era of discovery in which geographical and mental horizons expand beyond the globe. Francis Bacon (1561-1626) lays a foundation for modern science.

LA LUNA, or the Moon, is the title of the next card outlining history in the seventeenth century by the signs of cartomancy. The moon, obscured by dark clouds, sheds a pale twilight. In the distance are silhouettes of two towers. A dog and a wolf are baying at the moon. Tears or drops of blood fall from the face of the moon. A crawfish emerges from a pool in the foreground. This is the sinister picture that the ancient Egyptian priests drew when they watched the 17th century in their Magic Mirror. This is an excellent painting of the Thirty Years War (1618–1648) between the Catholic and Protestant countries which devastated Europe. Dogs and wolves bayed at the moon, and crawfish ate the dead bodies on the battlefields in those times. Blood and tears were shed—we can see them falling from the moon on this card. The plague broke out in England in 1665 and then four-fifths of London was destroyed in the Great Fire of 1666. This century saw the Civil War in England and the rule of Oliver Cromwell (1599-1658). This is all shown by symbols on the eighteenth Tarot card.

IL SOLE, or the Sun, is Card 19. A boy and a girl are playing in a garden in front of an unfinished wall. Tears drop from the dazzling sun. This Tarot card covers the eighteenth century. This is a painting of ancient Egyptian symbolists who gave us an image of the era of Louis XIV, the Sun-King. The wall may denote the construction of the Versailles Palace, splendid yet built at the cost of the sufferings of the common people of France. The sun with the drops means—splendour and tears. Figuratively, the boy and the girl may be Louis XVI with Marie-Antoinette playing innocently in the park of Versailles unaware of the coming storm of the French Revolution. This is the era of absolutism during which rule Peter the Great, Frederick the Great and Catherine the Great. Monarchical power reaches its apogee but this is only the calm before the storm. Louis XV said "after me—the deluge," and a deluge of blood was not far off.

IL GIUDIZIO, or the Judgment, is the name of the twentieth card. An angel with a trumpet soars in the clouds as three figures—a man, a woman and a child rise from an open grave. In this Script of Destiny of the ancients, the card illustrates the events of the 19th century. It is a perfect symbol of the Era of Revolution which began shortly before the dawn of the century with the burning of the Bastille in 1789, and the American Revolution from 1775 to 1789 when George Washington became the first President of the United States. The card depicts the rising of the Third Estate or the common people.

In France revolutions broke out in 1830, 1848 and 1871. Prussia and Austria experienced insurrections in 1848, and Italy in 1848 and 1860. The Paris Commune of 1871 echoed into the next century—it was a rehearsal for the Communist Revolution of Russia in 1917. Marxism, the gospel of the proletariat, appeared in this cycle of the *Last Judgment* and the *Rising of the Dead*.

The abolition of serfdom in Russia and of slavery in America took place in the second part of the 19th century —the century of the resurrection of the lower classes.

IL MATTO, or the Fool, is the next Tarot card.* A gaily-dressed, careless-looking man in a fool's cap is walking heedlessly into an abyss. A barking dog tries to grab

---

*Actually the card has no number but the French Masters of cartomancy—Dr. Gerard Encausse (Papus), Abbé Alphonse Louis Constant (Eliphas Levi), Christian Pitois (P. Christian) and others placed it before the last card.

him by the leg. The jester carries a stick and a bag. This is a cryptic forecast for the 20th century. The Fool is about to step over a precipice. This is not a particularly optimistic prophecy for our times, but it is true. This century has been defaced by two hideous, suicidal world wars. Never before in the whole history of mankind have wars been so costly and stupid. What does the Fool carry in his bag? A hydrogen-bomb that might trigger a chain reaction on the whole planet?

Man has become a fool because he has lost the evolutionary perspective of his journey through Time. It is ignorance and spiritual blindness that have driven him to the brink of the chasm. Perhaps we may learn something from Eastern apocrypha which contain a story about the fool:

"Once Jesus was seen walking down a road in great haste. People astonished at so unusual a behaviour, followed Him, asking: 'Why art Thou hurrying? Whom seekest Thou?' Jesus took no notice of them and continued on His way, hurrying. So they persistently cried: 'But in these places there are no wild beasts, no lions, panthers, wolves! What is it that is chasing Thee?' Then Jesus answered: 'I am running away from the fool!' 'But art not Thou the Christ? By the power of the Holy Ghost Thou canst blow on that man and he will become wise.' Jesus replied: 'By the breath of the Holy Spirit I can blow on the ignoramus and he will become all-knowing. I can breathe upon a blind man, and he will regain his sight. I breathe upon a dead man, and he comes back to life. But I breathe a thousand times upon the fool, and he still remains a fool—this is why I am running away from him.'"

However, the Epoch of the Fool is in its last stages as a better era is looming on the horizon.

One may reject the Egyptian origin of the Tarot on the

ground that the cards were generally unknown before 1300. But the striking similarity of the symbolical tablets with the events of the past seven hundred years can hardly be denied.

The DEVIL card is certainly a vivid picture of the Black Death which took a quarter of the population of Europe. Then there was another calamity—the Hundred Years War. The TOWER illustrates the shaken authority of royalty and papacy due to the appearance of secular literature. The STARS Tarot card predicts the age of astronomers. The MOON card with its dark night and crawfish eating the dead is the symbol of the Thirty Years War in the seventeenth century. In the SUN card one can recognise the era of the Sun-King and the building of Versailles. The tears dropping from the sun allegorise the sufferings of the overtaxed peasant and bourgeois of France. The JUDGMENT card anticipates the Century of Revolutions, and the liberation of the lower classes of society. It predicts the advent of democracy.

One may argue about our progress in technology in this push-button age. But it is still the era of the Fool, even a madman. Have we not drenched the planet in blood with this perfected technology? Have we not created a civilisation which, in the words of the American scientist Burstin, is defined as the "fun culture"? It is rather discomforting to know that the Fool may have a stockpile of atom-bombs in his bag.

In studying the prophecies of the Tarot scroll, one becomes convinced that the sages of antiquity had conquered Time and saw future events.

Now what is the shape of things to come according to the ciphered message of the Tarot cards?

In the Tarot cartomancy the last card IL MONDO, or The Universe, is a cryptogram for the 21st century. It depicts a virgin, in a garland, holding a wand, and walking on clouds. At the four corners of the card are the four signs of the zodiac—Aquarius, Scorpio, Leo and Taurus—in the symbology of a man, an eagle, a lion and a bull. The cosmic tone of this card is also emphasised by its name—the Universe.

No doubt this is Isis, the Egyptian Madonna. In the folklore of the land of the Nile, Isis found the severed parts of her slain husband Osiris and brought him to life. Allegorically, this may be a promise of the unification of the world. Mankind is on the threshold of this great cycle of Unity and Brotherhood. Isis, as the female protective principle of the universe, is thus described by Lucius Apuleius: "I am Nature, the universal Mother, mistress of all the elements, primordial child of Time." Under her protective influence an era of peace is certain to come.

Virgil must have known about the Egyptian Oracles as he wrote: "Here comes the Virgin's and Apollo's reign." In his Fourth Eclogue Virgil recorded the so-called Cumean Prophecy:

"The last era of Cumean song is now arrived and the grand series of ages begins afresh. Now the Virgin Astraea returns, and the reign of Saturn recommences. Now a new race descends from the celestial realms. Do thou, chaste Lucina, smile propitious to the infant boy who will bring to a close the present Age of Iron and introduce throughout the whole world the Age of Gold. Then shall the herds no longer dread the huge lion, the serpent also shall die and the poison's deceptive plant shall perish. Come then, dear child of the gods, great descendant of Jupiter! The time is near. See, the world is shaken with its globe saluting thee: the earth, the regions of the sea, and the heavens sublime."

It appears that the Roman sibyls as well as the initiate-priests of Egypt prophesied a Golden Age after the arrival of a "new race" from cosmic space. The Madonna on the twenty-second Tarot card is a promise of a better epoch which will rise soon.

20. NOSTRADAMUS—THE CONFIDANT OF KINGS

"I HAVE COME to see Nostradamus," curtly said four-teen-year-old Charles IX to assembled burghers of Salon-de-Provence on November 17, 1564, as they welcomed him, his brother Henry and Queen Catherine de Medici with an effusive speech.

Michel Nostradamus was born in St. Remy, Provence, in 1503. His grandfathers, Pierre de Nostradame and Jean de Saint-Remy, were Provençal Jews but Michel was baptised a Catholic. He received his degree at the University of Montpellier and became a physician. While the plague was raging in the south of France, he discovered a powder disinfectant, helped his patients, and became famous. Some biographers of Nostradamus call him the father of antiseptic medicine.

It was not Nostradamus's medical reputation that drew Charles IX to his doorstep but his celebrated astrological predictions. From boyhood Michel Nostradamus had a passion for astronomy and astrology. His learned grandfathers taught him these sciences and possibly that ancient scientific and philosophic tradition of the Hebrews known as the Cabbala. At a time when the heliocentric astronomy of Copernicus was hardly known and much condemned, Nostradamus bravely instructed his students on "the movements of the planets and the annual revolution of the earth around the sun."

In spite of his devout Catholicism Doctor Nostradamus was summoned by the Inquisitor at Agen to answer charges of heresy in 1538. Forewarned, Nostradamus hastily made arrangements to travel in another direction and thus missed the questioning.

The author feels that he is personally acquainted with Dr. Nostradamus because he has stood by his tomb in the church of St. Laurent in Salon and visited the house from which the prophet explored Time.

Many tales have survived testifying to the extraordinary gift of seership which Michel Nostradamus possessed. Once he met a monk in Italy who had been a swineherd in his native village. Nostradamus fell on his knees before the humble monk Felix Peretti and accosted him as "Your Holiness" to the amusement of fellow-monks. Decades later, the young friar became Cardinal of Montalto and then Pope Sixtus V.

It is for his *Centuries*, first published in 1555, that Dr. Nostradamus became renowned throughout the world. The twelve *Centuries* contain about one thousand two hundred verses of prophecies in garbled archaic French. I have used the Pierre Chevillot edition of the *Centuries* issued in Troyes in 1611 which incorporates the earlier versions of Mace Bonhomme (1555), Antoine du Rosne (1557), Barbe Regnault (1560) and Rigaud (1568).

Although the stanzas are readable, their meaning is often impossible to understand. Nostradamus admitted this in his letter to King Henry II: "But some may answer that the rhyme is as easy to understand as to blow one's nose, but the sense is more difficult to grasp."

In the same letter Dr. Michel Nostradamus even claimed that he "could have set down in every quatrain the exact time in which they (events) shall happen, but it would not please everybody and much less the interpretation of them."

The reason for veiling his predictions in enigmatic sentences was explained by Nostradamus himself in the Preface to the *Centuries*: "If I came to refer to that which will be in the future, those of the realm, sect, religion and faith would find it so poorly in accord with their petty

111

fancies that they would come to condemn that which future ages shall know and understand to be true."

This ever-present opposition from the establishment led him to "show by abstruse and twisted sentences the future causes, even the most urgent, as I perceived them, whatever changes might be, so only as not to scandalise their fragile hearing, and write down everything under a figure rather cloudy than plainly prophetic."

In the introduction to the *Centuries* Nostradamus mentions occult philosophy. Did he inherit some rare manuscripts of great antiquity from his grandfathers? This is a reasonable supposition supported by his own confession in the Epistle to his son César: "Many volumes which have been hidden for centuries have come before my eyes. But dreading what might happen in the future, having read them, I presented them to Vulcan, and as the fire began to devour them the flame, licking the air, shot forth an unaccustomed brightness, clearer than natural flame, like the flash from an explosive powder casting a strange illumination over the house."

In a house near the Tour de l'Horloge in Salon-de-Provence, Nostradamus began systematically to record his "trips in Time". A spiral staircase led to a top room reserved for his unearthly pursuits. His privacy was well protected by his loving wife, Anne Ponsart Gemelle, and faithful disciple, Jean Aymes de Chavigny, who wrote *La Vie et le Testament de Michel Nostradamus*.

In the opening verses of the *Centuries* Nostradamus reveals the technique of his nocturnal visits into the future. He used a brass tripod, wand, water and a flame to induce a special state described by de Chavigny as "plein d'un enthousiasme et comme ravi d'une fureur toute novelle," that is, a state of trance.

The Theory of Relativity proves the connection between mass, energy, the speed of light and Time. Time will shrink in a photon spaceship as atomic processes slow down on a fast space voyage. Upon return to Earth after this flight the astronauts will find themselves in another century. Were the cells of Nostradamus's body made to vibrate slower to gain Time in a jump into the future?

Only a small number of stanzas contain dates. As the *Centuries* were not arranged by Nostradamus in chronological order, it is often impossible to connect his predictions with historical incidents. However, some verses are so clear that the events which Nostradamus anticipated in the future can be easily identified.

An attempt to introduce chronology in the *Centuries* has been made by Roger Frontenac, the discoverer of the *hyperbolic key* to the quatrains by means of which every stanza can be dated.* Frontenac scores many direct hits but certain stanzas such as 9.18 already identified with an historical event, are obviously misdated. Roger Frontenac's mathematical calculations are not faulty. Perhaps Nostradamus purposely complicated his method of coding.

In this chapter the Key of Frontenac is used mainly as a double check on the identification of events. We shall begin with Century 9, Quatrain 49, which, according to Frontenac, pertains to the year 1650:

Senat de Londres mettront a mort leur Roy. (9.49)
(The Parliament of London will put to death its King.)

In 1649 the English Parliament condemned Charles I to death—the one and only execution of a king in the history of England.

Le sang du juste à Londres fera faute,
Brulez par foudres de vingt trois les six. (2.51)
(The blood of the just shall be lacking in London,
burnt by fireballs in three score and six.)

*R. Frontenac, *La Clef Secrète de Nostradamus*, Paris, 1950.

Nostradamus was a notorious royalist and he thought that London would be punished for killing Charles I. Three words attract attention—*London, Fire* and *Sixty-six*. The prophecy was fulfilled—the city of London was burned by the Great Fire in 1666.

The sage of Provence gave convincing predictions of coming events in the history of France.

Quand le fourcheu sera soustenu de deux paux,
Avec six demy corps, et six ciseaux ouvers:
Le tres puissant seigneur, heritier des crapaux,
Alors subjuguera sous soy tout l'univers. (10.101)
(When the fork will be supported by two pillars,
With six half-horns and six open scissors:
The very powerful Lord, heir of the toads,
Then will bring the whole world into subjection to
    himself.)

The quatrain is not as nonsensical as it looks. A fork with two pillars is M or 1000, six half-horns or CCCCCC is 600, and six open scissors or XXXXXX is 60. The total is 1660—a definite date. In 1660 Louis XIV, the heir to the toads, the insignia of the Merovingians and then of the kings of France, personally took over the rule of France while Cardinal Mazarin was dying. He became the Grand Monarch, the most powerful king of Europe.

There is a quatrain which the author will endeavour to decipher in view of a precise date:

Croistra le nombre si grand des astronomes,
Chassez, bannis et livres censurez,
L'an mil six cent et sept par sacre glomes
Que nul aux sacres ne seront asseurez. (8.71)

(The number of astronomers will so increase
That they will be punished, banished and their books
    censured,

114

By ecclesiastical assemblies in the year 1607,
That none at holy rites shall be secure.)

Nostradamus anticipated the Age of Science and the persecution of its pioneers. Now let us review the activities of the astronomers at about 1607. First of all, Giordano Bruno was burned at the stake in 1600. A nova appeared in 1604 and was visible until 1606. This gave Galileo the pretext to challenge the age-old Aristotelian concept of the "incorruptibility of the heavens." The Dutchman Lippershey discovered the principles of the telescope in 1608 while Galileo constructed one in 1609. The Milky Way resolved itself into stars, spots were found on the sun, craters on the moon, satellites around Jupiter, precipitating a revolution in science. The Church condemned astrology at the Council of Malines in 1607 and banned the Copernican Theory by an Index in 1616.

Kepler began to formulate his three famous laws of astronomy in 1607. This great astronomer was persecuted. A relative was burned as a witch before his eyes. His aged mother died in chains in prison. Perhaps Nostradamus watched all these frightful scenes from a tripod in his house in Salon. Most of these "purges" of astronomers took place around 1607, as he said.

The prophet of Provence predicted no important changes for France until the end of the 18th century. But for England he foretold seven changes in three centuries:

Sept fois changer verrez gens Britannique,
Taints en sang en deux cens nonante an,
Franchenon point. (3.57)
(Seven times the people of Britain will see change
Bloodstained for 290 years,
Not France.)

Historically, this is correct. In 1532 Henry VIII broke with Rome. In 1553 Mary Stuart re-established the

Catholic Church in England, in 1558 Elizabeth I banned the Catholics. In 1649 Charles I was beheaded and in 1660 came the restoration of Charles II. In 1689 James II was dethroned by William III, and in 1714 the reign of the House of Hanover was established.

Le grand empire sera par Angleterre
Le Pempotam des ans plus de trois cens. (10.100)
(The great empire of England
will be all powerful for more than three centuries.)

When Nostradamus wrote these lines England was one of the less important countries in Europe rather than a "great empire". In 1588, thirty-three years after the Book of Prophecies of Nostradamus had been published, England defeated the Spanish Armada. The power of Britain did last for "more than three centuries" to the end of World War I, when America rose as the dominant power. This take-over was foretold by the Prophet of Salon in another verse:

Le chef de Londres, par regne d'Americh. (10.66)
(The chief of London, ruled by America.)

This line portends the economic dependence of London on America which is an accomplished fact now.

The American Revolution was also prophesied by Nostradamus:

Le recogneu passer le bas, puis haut
L'Occident libres les Isles Britanniques. (7.S-2)
(The recognised ones pass low, then high,
The West freed of the British Isles.)

This is a prediction of the independence gained by the American colonies from the British Isles and the eventual ascendancy of the United States of America.

116

There is another verse in the *Centuries* which is thought
to allude to America, too:

Dans l'aquatique triplicité naistra,
D'un qui fera Jeudy pour sa feste:
Son bruit, loz, regne, sa puissance croistra,
Par Terre et Mer, aux Oriens tempeste. (1.50)
(From the aquatic triplicity shall be born,
One who shall make Thursday his feast day,
His fame, praise, rule and power shall grow
By Land and Sea, and storm the Orient.)

The only nation which celebrates Thursday—the last
Thursday in November, or Thanksgiving Day, is the
United States. It is a "feast day" with the inevitable turkey
on the table. North America was populated by colonists
who came in English, Dutch and French ships, and this
may be the "aquatic triplicity" Nostradamus speaks of. He
is right about the fame and power of the new nation—the
U.S.A. Neither is he wrong about America storming the
Orient—it began with Admiral Perry pointing the guns of
his ships at Yokohama in 1854 and repeated itself in the
20th century with the fighting by American troops in
Japan, Korea and Vietnam.

The 18th quatrain of the *9th Century* can serve as an
example of Nostradamus's clear visions of the future veiled
in obscure sentences:

Le Lys Dauffois portera dans Nansi
Jusques en Flandres electeur de l'Empire,
Neufve obturée au grand Montmorency,
Hors lieux provez delivre à clere peine. (9.18)
(The Lily of the Dauphin will be carried to Nancy,
Even to Flandres, an Elector of the Empire,
New prison to the great Montmorency,

117

Away from the customary place, delivered to his clear
    punishment.)

Louis XIII, the bearer of the royal lilies, entered Nancy
on September 24, 1633. Two years later, when the Elector
of Trèves was imprisoned by the Spaniards, Louis XIII
declared war on Spain and marched into Flanders.

The last two lines are even more striking. The Duke of
Montmorency, Marshal of France and Viceroy of Canada,
was convicted of treason in 1632 and condemned to death.
As a concession to his high rank, Cardinal Richelieu
promised that he would not be beheaded in the public
square of Toulouse, or the "customary place", but would
be executed in the prison courtyard. Richelieu also per-
mitted the services of the executioner (Monsieur de Paris)
to be dispensed with. A simple soldier from the ranks
drawn by lot was chosen for the execution, and his name
was Clerepeyne—the last two words in the quatrain!

Had the Seer of Provence written only—*Dauphin, Nancy,
Flandres, Elector, Montmorency* and *Clerepeyne*—the
names still would have made sense to an historian. It is evident that Nostradamus saw three-dimensional Technicolor
films of history before they were projected on the screen
of Time.

Nostradamus's prophecies of the French Revolution are
uncannily accurate. In a letter to King Henry II, written
on June 27, 1558, he predicts anti-Church riots: "It shall
be in the year 1792 at which time everyone will think it a
renovation of the age."

The Revolution was born out of anti-clerical teachings.
The Republic of France was established on September 25,
1792. There was nothing ambiguous in the prophecy of
the Provençal astrologer.

In his *Epistle to César*, his son, Nostradamus refers to
L'avènement du Commun, or the Advent of the Commons,

118

that is the triumph of democracy which he expected in a future century.

The famous *Varennes Prophecy* is enigmatic but true. In Frontenac's Key it is placed in the year 1790 which is uncannily accurate.

De nuict viendra par la forest de Reines
Deux pars voultprie Herne la pierre blanche,
Le moine noir en gris dedans Varennes
Esleu cap. cause tempeste, feu, sang, tranche. (9.20)
(By night will come through the forest of Rheims
Two married persons by circuitous route, the Queen, the white stone,
The monkish king in grey at Varennes.
The Elected Capet will cause tempest, fire, blood, beheading.)

Nostradamus frequently employed anagrams. *Herne* stands for *Reine*, or the Queen, and *cap.* for Capet (the dynasty of the kings of France), *noir en gris* for Roi en gris (king in grey).

On June 20, 1791, the flight of Louis XVI and Marie-Antoinette took place. The Queen was dressed in white on that summer night while the king was clad in grey so as not to attract attention. They proceeded in the great coach by a circuitous route to the border. At one town the king put his head out of the carriage and was recognised. Further down the road at the village of Varennes, the royal couple was arrested and taken to Paris. On January 21, 1793, Louis Capet was guillotined and many were to follow him in this orgy of "sang tranche" or bloody beheading as Nostradamus called it, 236 years before it happened.

La pierre blanche has been interpreted as an allusion to the Affair of the Diamond Necklace, involving Cardinal Rohan and the Countess de Lamotte who stole it. The Queen's unpopularity was increased by the scandal.

In another quatrain the great Time explorer of Salon-de-Provence draws two scenes—one at the Tuileries and the other at Varennes:

Le part soluz mary sera mitte
Retour conflict passera sur le thuille:
Par cinq sens un trahyr sera tiltre
Narbon et Saulce par contaux avons d'huille. (9.34)
(The husband alone will be mitred.
Return: a conflict will pass over the Tiles (the
    Tuileries)
By the five hundred. A traitor will be titled
Narbon, and from Saulce we have oil in quarts.)

In chronological order the last two lines should come first. The Count de Narbonne was the most influential minister at this time of crisis and he played a double role. Sauce was the mayor of Varennes who stopped the royal cortège from escaping from France and received 20,000 pounds from the National Assembly as a reward. He was a dealer in oil.

The first part of the verse is equally clear. On June 20, 1792, exactly one year after the king's detention at Varennes, the Jacobins staged a mass demonstration and stormed the Tuileries Palace. They put their red cap (mitre) on Louis XVI. The Queen was not present at the time and "the husband alone will be mitred" prophecy came true.

"Return: a conflict will pass over the Tiles (the Tuileries) by the five hundred," continues the clairvoyant of Salon. Five hundred revolutionary troops returned on August 10, 1792, slew the Swiss Guards, occupied the Tuileries and deposed the king. The very mention of the Tuileries Palace is extraordinary—the building did not exist when Nostradamus lived!

It must be noted here that from the first to the last page

of the *Centuries* Michel Nostradamus always tries to show his royalist sentiments and devotion to the Catholic Church —probably in order to avoid persecution.

His Napoleonic prophecies are famous for their veracity:

Un empereur naistra pres d'Italie,
Qui à l'Empire sera vendu bien cher,
Diront avec quels gens il se ralie,
Qu'on trouvera moins prince que boucher. (1.60)
(An emperor will be born near Italy
Who will cost the empire dear,
When it is seen with what people he allies himself,
He will be found less a prince than a butcher.)

It is apparent that Nostradamus expected the birth of Napoleon Bonaparte in Corsica, a place "near Italy". Faithful to the crowned rulers of France, he is critical of the coming emperor. In another passage of the *Centuries* Nostradamus depicts Napoleon's spectacular rise:

De soldat simple parviendra en empire,
De robe courte parviendra à ia longue:
Vaillant aux armes en eglise ou plus pyre,
Vexer les prestres comme l'eau fait l'esponge. (8.57)
(From being a simple soldier he will attain to an empire,
From the short robe he will attain to a long one,
Valiant in arms, in the church, where at his worst,
He will vex the clergy as water does the sponge.)

The quatrain dated by Frontenac as 1800 hardly needs any comment because of its clarity. The short robe is Napoleon's consular attire, and the long one is his imperial mantle. The emperor's military successes are in the prophecy as well as his conflicts with the Church.

Napoleon Bonaparte's Russian campaign seems to have been foreseen by Nostradamus:

Amas s'approche venant d'Esclavonie,
L'Olestant vieux cité ruynera.
Fort desolée verra Romanie,
Puis la grand' flamme estaindra ne scaura. (4.82)
(A great mass of men approach, coming from the land
  of the Slavs,
The Destroyer will ruin the old city,
Not knowing how to extinguish the great flame,
Most unhappy to see his Rome vanish.)

Whenever Notradamus mentions *Esclave* or *Escla-*
vonie he means Russia. To Poland he directly refers as
such. In his time Slavic countries were under Turkish or
Austrian rule. The meaning of this quatrain is not difficult
to decipher. In 1812 Napoleon I occupied Moscow which
was set afire in an uncontrollable conflagration. The great
mass of men is the *Grande Armée* in retreat from Russia
in one of the coldest winters on record. This ruined the
Emperor's dream of becoming the ruler of the Western
and Eastern Roman Empires.

Nostradamus even counted the years during which
Napoleon would be in power:

De la cité marine et tributaire,
La teste raze prendra la satrapie:
Chasser sordide qui puis sera contraire,
Par quatorze ans tiendra la tyrannie. (7.13)
(Of the maritime city and tributary,
The man with short hair shall assume governorship:
He will chase away the mercenaries who will oppose
  him later,
For fourteen years shall he hold tyranny.)

Napoleon Bonaparte, a man with short hair as compared
with the wigged men of the previous years, took the port
of Toulon from the English, a commercial, mercenary

nation that fought him later. He held absolute power for fourteen years from 1799 to 1814.

Some interpreters of Nostradamus's *Centuries* believe that the following verse may allude to the 1914-1918 War:

L'horrible guerre qu'en l'Occident s'appreste,
L'an ensuivant viendra la pestilence
Si fort horrible, que jeune, vieux ne beste,
Sang, feu—Mercure, Mars, Jupiter en France. (9.55)
(A terrible war is in store for the West,
The year following shall come the pestilence,
So strangely terrible that young, old, nor beast (shall escape),
Blood, fire—Mercury, Mars, Jupiter in France.)

In 1914 Mercury, Mars and Jupiter entered Leo, traditionally the house of France, between May and August. The pestilence which ravaged Europe during and after World War I was Spanish influenza, taking a toll almost equal to that of the war itself.

The *Centuries* contain a quatrain which is generally taken for a prediction of the construction of the tragic Maginot Line (the year 1940 according to the *Hyperbolic Key*):

Pres du grand fleuve grand fosse, terre egeste
En quinze pars sera l'eau divisée:
La cité prinse, fue, sang, cris, conflict mettre (4.80)
(Near the great river a mighty fortress is hollowed out of the earth;
It will divide the stream into fifteen segments:
The conflict puts the captured city to fire, blood, cries.)

The Maginot Line system of fortifications stretched from Switzerland to Luxembourg along the *great river*, the Rhine. Underground fortifications were divided into fifteen main sectors and Nostradamus must have counted them on his trip into the future. German Panzer divisions outflanked the Maginot Line and occupied Paris on June 14, 1940.

Another prophecy of the Provençal astrologer can be interpreted as a scene of night bombing and shelling in the 20th century:

Sera laisse feu vif, mort caché,
Dedans les globes horrible espouvantable,
De nuict a classe cité en poudre lasché,
La cité a feu, l'ennemy favorable. (5.8)
(There will be loosed living fire, death hidden,
In the horrible, frightful globes,
By night hostile forces will reduce the city to powder,
A burnt city—an advantage to the enemy.)

Reading this verse, one thinks of Rotterdam, Coventry, Warsaw, Minsk and Kiev destroyed during World War II. Michel Nostradamus must have studied the manœuvres of aeroplanes taking off from aerodromes or aircraft carriers, and attacking from the air against all "laws of warfare".

Les saturelles terre et mer vent propice,
Prins, mort, troussez, pillez, sans loys de guerre. (3.82)
(Grasshoppers by land and sea, the wind being propitious,
Capture, death, pursuit, plunder without laws of warfare.)

Lawless "grasshoppers" may be Nostradamus's name for air raiders flying over land and sea.

The learned doctor of Provence did not omit the Russian Revolution:

Le gent esclave par heurt martial,
Viendra en haur degré tant eslevée,

Changeront Prince, naistra un Provincial,
Passer la mer copie aux monts levée. (5.26)
(The Slavic people in a martial hour,
Will become in a high degree so uplifted:
They will change their sovereign, for a provincial,
Pass the sea, army from raised mountains.)

When Nostradamus speaks of *esclaves*, he usually means the Russians. The February Revolution of 1917 removed the Czar while Russia was still engaged in World War I. The October Revolution put Lenin at the head of the state. He was born in Simbirsk and educated in Kazan—both provincial towns. Many years of his life were spent abroad. Lenin left alpine Switzerland on April 9, 1917, passed Germany in a sealed carriage under army surveillance, then crossed the Baltic Sea on the way to Stockholm. Seven days later he arrived at Petrograd to lead the revolution. The last words of the quatrain are a reference to the mountains of Switzerland where Lenin lived.

Another verse contains a definite prediction of the Nazi campaigns:

De la partie de Mammer grand Pontife,
Subjuguera les confine du Danube:
Chasser les crois, par fer rasse ne risse,
Captifs, or, bagues plus de cent mille rubes. (6.49)
(By the project of Mammon's high priest,
They shall subjugate the borders of the Danube,
They shall pursue iron 'topsy-turvy' crosses,
Captives, gold, jewels, more than a hundred thousand
   rubles.)

When Germany's "Mammon" or big business assured Hitler of financial support, he began his eastward march across Czechoslovakia, down the Danube towards Russia.

125

Wherever the iron swastikas ("topsy-turvy crosses") rolled, industries and banks were confiscated, and men and women sent to labour camps. The Nazi invasion of Russia is suggested by the word rubles—the Russian currency.

A verse in the *Centuries* can be taken as an indication of Nostradamus's knowledge of the atomic bombing of Hiroshima in the land of the Rising Sun:

Soleil levant un grand feu l'on verra,
Bruit et clarte vers Aquilon tendants.
Dedans le rond mort et cris l'on orra,
Par glaive feu, faim, mort les attendants. (2.91)
(In the rising sun a great fire shall be seen,
Noise and brightness towards the north.
Within the circle, death, and cries shall be heard,
By sword, fire, hunger, death awaits.)

On the morning of August 6, 1945, history was made—the first atomic bomb was used in warfare. The *Enola Gay* bomber flew at 9,588 metres when the awful bomb was released. The plane came from the Tinian Island near Guam, and its course was north-west, or *towards the north.* There was a roar and brightness from the *great fire* in the land of the *Rising Sun.* Within the circle of radiation—death and destruction. The maimed, burnt by radioactive contamination, unable to swallow food, starved to death. All these ghastly scenes are described by Nostradamus.

Those who favour the coincidence theory in explaining Nostradamus should hear the story about a boy who was once asked by a teacher: "If you fall from the leaning tower of Pisa and remain alive, what is that?" "Good fortune, sir," answered the schoolboy. "What if you fall again and stay alive? How would you define that?" asked the teacher. "A coincidence," replied the lad. "Imagine you fall from the tower a third time and are still alive—what would you call that?" interrogated the examiner. "That would be a habit, sir," replied the boy.

Apparently, the prophet of Provence made a habit of coincidental predictions.

Did the wise doctor of Salon-de-Provence know what is in store for us? The answer is contained in the Epistle to his son César in which he says: "I have made books of prophecies, each one containing a hundred astronomical stanzas which I have joined obscurely, and are perpetual predictions from this year (1555) to the year 3797."

It is not an easy task to identify the stanzas belonging to our century. Only in one quatrain Nostradamus dated an event in this century—the year 1999. Nonetheless, in the dedicatory letter to his son he says that "we are now in the seventh millenary which ends all and brings us near the eighth." It is reasonable to think that the next, or the eighth-millennium begins in the year 2000 in Nostradamian chronology.

In the puzzling quatrains of the *Centuries* as well as in the letter to his son, Nostradamus writes about a future geological cataclysm: "Before the universal conflagration shall happen so many great inundations that there shall scarce be any land that shall not be covered with water, and this shall last so long, that except for ethnographies and topographies all shall perish. Before and after these inundations in many countries there shall be such scarcity of rain and such a great deal of fire, and burning stones shall fall from heaven, that nothing unconsumed shall be left."

To our great relief Nostradamus overlooked dating this universal conflagration, flood and meteoric bombardment.

Michel Nostradamus is a master of the impossible—he claims that two suns will shine in our system in a distant future:

Le grand estoile par sept jours bruslera,
Nuee fera deux soleils apparoir, (2.41)
(The great star for seven days shall burn,
A cloud shall make two suns appear.)

The great star may be a comet as enormous as the apparent size of the sun. Let us recall the celebrated comet of 1811 which was larger than the sun's disc. Only a science-fiction fan may be able to accept this and other incredible things Nostradamus wrote about.

L'an mil neuf cens nonante neuf sept mois,
Du ciel viendra un grand Roy d'effrayeur. (10.72)
(In the year 1999 and seven months,
From the sky will come an alarmingly powerful King.)

If space visitors are coming in 1999, they may establish peace on earth. This is exactly what Nostradamus says in the following verse with the date of 2080 in Frontenac's list:

La règne humain d'Anglique geniture,
Fera son règne paix union tenir:
Captive guerre demy de sa closture,
Long temps la paix leur fera maintenir. (10.42)
(The human reign of angelic origin,
Shall cause his reign to be in peace and union,
Shall make war captive, shutting it half up,
Will make them keep peace for a long time.)

It is possible that our suicidal attempts to blow up Planet 3 of the solar system will compel a "galactic patrol" to stop them.

Although Nostradamus speaks of vast changes in the apocalyptic times at the end of the 20th century, he closes on a cheerful note. In the letter to his son in the *Centuries* he writes: "After this has lasted a certain time, there almost will be renewed another reign of Saturn, a golden age."

21. ST. MALACHY AND THE VATICAN

THE DOMINICAN MONK Arnold de Wion published his *Lignum Vitae* in Venice in 1595. It concerns prophecies about the future Popes by St. Malachy, Bishop of Armagh, Northern Ireland, who lived in the 12th century. De Wion claimed that the manuscript of the Irish bishop was examined by Pope Innocent II and approved for preservation in the Vatican archives. According to Arnold de Wion, the document had been kept at the Vatican for almost five centuries before he obtained it. Printing was still an innovation in Wion's times, and the Vatican censors examined all material for publication before granting their approval. Therefore, the manuscript must be historically authentic.

Although St. Malachy predicted all future Popes from the 12th century onwards, we are on firm ground only from the date of publication of *Lignum Vitae* (1595).

It was St. Bernard de Clairvaux who had written about St. Malachy and vouched for his gift of prophecy. He was an intimate friend of St. Malachy who died in St. Bernard's arms in 1148.

It is highly significant that St. Bernard was one of the founders of the Order of the Temple. In a former chapter we established a link between the Tarotic Scroll of Time and the Templars. A similar connection exists between St. Malachy's Prophecies and the Order of the Temple as if the Templar Chiefs had possessed the secret of breaking the Time Barrier.

Friar de Wion wrote an introduction to his book stating that "St. Malachy has himself written some small works which I have not seen, excepting only a certain prophecy concerning the Sovereign Pontiffs; as it is brief, and has not yet, so far as I know, been printed, and since many desire to be acquainted with it, we have reproduced it here."

Seven printed pages contain 111 mottoes of future Popes by means of which they could later be identified. St. Malachy's roll of Popes was first printed in 1595 on the five-hundredth anniversary of his birth. All prophecies before that date will be omitted. But the 35 remaining papal devices, covering a period of 400 years from 1600 to 2000, deserve an unbiased examination.

The prophecies of St. Malachy received a wide circulation during the pontificate of Clement VIII (1592-1605).

UNDOSUS VIR, or WAVE MAN, is the prophetic device for the next Pope. It was an astonishingly true prediction for Leo XI who reigned for only twenty-seven days in 1605—he passed like a wave.

GENS PERVERSA, or PERVERSE PEOPLE is the descriptive phrase for the following Pope. Paul V (1605-1621) was his name and he had difficulties with the Protestants, who in the Catholic terminology of St. Malachy were "perverse people".

IN TRIBULATIONE PACIS, or IN THE TRIBULATION OF PEACE, is the code for Pope Gregory XV (1621-1623). As an Apostolic Nuncio he established peace between Savoy, France and Spain, troubled by wars.

LILIUM ET ROSA, or the LILY AND THE ROSE, stands for Urban VIII (1623-1644). It is not difficult to guess why St. Malachy used the symbology of flowers in this case. Pope Urban VIII gave dispensation for the marriage of Henrietta of France, whose coat-of-arms was the lilies, to Charles I of England, whose badge was the rose.

JUCUNDITAS CRUCIS, or THE JOY OF THE CROSS, is the prophecy for the next Pope, whose name was Innocent X (1644-1655). He was raised to the pontificate on the Feast of the Exaltation of the Cross.

MONTIUM CUSTOS, or the GUARDIAN OF THE HILLS, is the cryptogram for the next Pope in St. Malachy's prophecies. He was Alexander VII who occupied the Papal throne from 1655 to 1667. The coat of arms of the family of Fabio-Chigi, to which he belonged, featured a star suspended over six hills.

SYDUS OLORUM, or THE STAR OF THE SWANS, is the next motto. It stands for Pope Clement IX (1667-1669), who was born in Pistoia, the emblem of which is a star. Pope Clement IX usually held his conclaves in the Chamber of the Swans. The prophecy was uncanny in its accuracy.

DE FLUMINE MAGNO, or FROM THE MIGHTY RIVER, is the code for the next Pope—Clement X (1670-1676). In his infancy he was almost swept away by the mighty Tiber at floodtide. It is also significant that the armorial device of Altieri, that is of the Pope, shows the Milky Way or *Magnum flumen*—the mighty river.

BELLUA INSATIABILIS, or the INSATIABLE BEAST, is the enigmatic prophecy for the following Pope —Innocent XI (1676-1689). A lion with an eagle are displayed on the escutcheon of the Odescalchi family to which the Pope belonged.

POENITENTIA GLORIOSA, or GLORIOUS PENITENCE, is next in the list of St. Malachy. The Keys of St. Peter were then held by Alexander VIII (1689-1691). After King Louis XIV of France had surrendered Avignon to the Papacy, the Pope coined a commemorative medal with a motto *Poenitentia Gloriosa*—the exact words of St. Malachy.

RASTRUM IN PORTA, or THE RAKE IN THE PORT, is the strange slogan of the next Pope—Innocent XII (1691-1700). His birthplace was the port of Naples, and the coat of arms of Pignatelli del Rastello displays a rake.

FLORES CIRCUMDATI, or ENCIRCLED BY FLOWERS, stands for Pope Clement XI (1700-1721), who was born in Urbino, Italy, the insignia of which shows a garland of flowers.

DE BONA RELIGIONE, or OF GOOD RELIGION, is the puzzling prophecy for the next Pope, as if he could be otherwise. The successor of Clement XI was Innocent XIII (1721-1724), from the family of Conti which had given six Popes to the Church. This explains the enigmatic code of St. Malachy.

MILES IN BELLO, or SOLDIER IN BATTLE, is the code-name of the next Pope—Benedict XIII (1724-1730), descended from the soldier clan of Orsini.

COLUMNA EXCELSA, or LOFTY COLUMN, predicts the following Pope—Clement XII (1730-1740). He was greatly interested in architecture and built a chapel at St. John Lateran's, where he used two ancient Roman columns from the Pantheon of Agrippa. He meant to be interred in the chapel.

ANIMAL RURALE, or THE RURAL ANIMAL, is the device for Pope Benedict XIV (1740-1758). He came from a rural district. Also, he had a reputation of "working like an ox" having written many volumes.

ROSA UMBRIAE, or THE ROSE OF UMBRIA, is St. Malachy's prophetic message for the next Pope—Clement XIII (1758-1769) who, before his election, had been the governor of Rieti in Umbria. The rose is the badge of that city.

URSUS VELOX, or THE SWIFT BEAR, is the device

for the next Pontiff—Clement XIV (1769-1774). The shield of the family of Ganganelli, to which he belonged, shows a bear rampant.

PEREGRINUS APOSTOLICUS, or THE PILGRIM POPE, is the peculiar phrase describing the successor of Clement XIV—Pope Pius VI (1775-1799). At the end of his pontificate in those revolutionary times he had to leave Rome and died in exile.

AQUILA RAPAX, or THE RAPACIOUS EAGLE, portrays the Pope in the Napoleonic era—Pius VII (1800-1823). St. Malachy used an historical background to describe the Pontiff. The *Rapacious Eagle* refers, of course, to the standard of Napoleon I.

CANIS ET COLUBER, or A DOG AND A SERPENT, stand for Pope Leo XII (1823-1829), who was known for vigilance and wisdom. According to Lenfant, the Pope's escutcheon of della Genga was emblazoned with a dog and a snake.*

VIR RELIGIOSUS, or THE MAN OF RELIGION, is an odd name for a Pope. His name was Pius VIII (1829-1830), and the only encyclical he issued was *Laxity in Religion.*

DE BALNEIS ETRURIA, or FROM THE BATHS OF ETRURIA, is the prophecy for the next Pope. Gregory XVI (1831-1846) was a member of the Order of Camaldolese founded in Balneum (Baths), Etruria.

CRUX DE CRUCE, or CROSS FROM A CROSS, is another puzzling name intended by St. Malachy to identify the next Pope—Pius IX (1846-1878). He was tormented or 'crucified' by the House of Savoy, the emblem of which is a cross.

LUMEN IN COELO, or LIGHT IN THE SKY, is the motto identifying the next Pontiff—Leo XIII (1878-1903). Apparently, the sentence alludes to the coat-of-arms of

*C. Lenfant, *Le Dernier Siècle*, Bordeaux, c. 1900.

the Pecci family which bears a golden shooting star on an azure field.

IGNIS ARDENS, or BURNING FIRE, is the prophetic rubric for Pope Pius X (1903-1914). It was in his reign that World War I broke out. That conflagration was a *Burning Fire*, indeed.

RELIGIO DEPOPULATA, or DEPOPULATED RELIGION, stands for Benedict XV (1914-1922) in St. Malachy's roll of future Popes. The device refers to the millions of Christians killed in World War I as well as to the Russian Revolution which severed Russia from Christianity.

FIDES INTERPIDA, or UNSHAKEN FAITH, is the rubric for the next Pontiff—Pius XI (1922-1939). He had many embarrassments in trying to maintain Catholicism in Mexico and Spain, but preserved his faith.

PASTOR ANGELICUS, or THE ANGELIC POPE, is the descriptive title given by St. Malachy to Pope Pius XII (1939-1958), who was mystically inclined and experienced visions.

PASTOR ET NAUTA, or SHEPHERD AND PILOT, the ciphered prediction of St. Malachy to identify the next Pope—John XXIII (1958-1963)—has never been explained. But it is not difficult to grasp the meaning of *Shepherd and Pilot* when we realise the completely new course that the Pope charted for the Church. Does it also mean "the Pope in the age of ASTOR ET NAUTA, or ASTRONAUTICS, which was born in the reign of John XXIII?

FLOS FLORUM, or THE FLOWER OF FLOWERS, is another unsolved device which stands for the present Pope Paul VI (1963-). St. Malachy's motto may allude to the emblem of the United Nations Organisation, a disc in a wreath, divided into eight sectors, with concentric circles and outlines of continents. On the background of this "eight-petalled flower" the Pope delivered his memorable address in the U.N. General Assembly in 1965—the first of its kind in history. On the other hand, Paul VI was the only cardinal in the Sacred College whose coat-of-arms displayed flowers—the lilies.

One can be critical about the opinions of commentators in regard to some of St. Malachy's prophecies. However, ROSA UMBRIAE which represented Pope Clement XIII who came from Umbria with its emblem—the rose—is a striking prophecy. So is AQUILA RAPAX for Pius VII, the Pope during the reign of Napoleon Bonaparte, whose standard was the eagle. The device for Gregory XVI reads DE BALNEIS ETRURIA. It is amazingly true—the Pope was a member of the Camaldolese Order, founded in Balneum, Etruria. LUMEN IN COELO is a direct reference to the comet on the blue shield of Leo XIII.

It is difficult to explain these predictions by coincidence. St. Malachy predicted momentous events for the end of the 20th century. According to him only four more Popes will ascend the throne of St. Peter. St. Malachy gave the following identifying mottoes to the remaining Popes:

DE MEDIETATE LUNAE, or CONCERNING THE HALF-MOON;

DE LABORE SOLIS, or OF THE LABOUR OF THE SUN;

DE GLORIA OLIVAE, or OF THE GLORY OF THE OLIVE;

PETRO ROMANO, or PETER THE ROMAN, the last Pope.

It has been estimated that the average reign of each Pope lasts about eight years. Therefore, the terms of these four Popes should cover a period of approximately thirty-two years from the transition of the present Pope Paul VI.

The personalities of future Pontiffs are described by St. Malachy by enigmatic devices. CONCERNING THE

135

HALF-MOON suggests a connection with events in the Mohammedan world at the time, or even the moon itself during a space probe. OF THE LABOUR OF THE SUN may refer to intensive solar activity during the reign of the future Pope. DE GLORIA OLIVAE has been interpreted as a papal reign of peace but it may have another meaning. The prophecy of St. Malachy concerning the last Pope whom he calls PETER THE ROMAN says that he will rule in the midst of tribulations culminating in the destruction of Papacy.

22. ROERICH—PROPHECIES IN COLOUR

IT WAS MAXIM GORKY who called Nicholas Roerich "the greatest intuitivist of modern life." Roerich created some five thousand paintings found in leading museums and art collections all over the world.

A certain number of his works of art have a pronounced motif of prophecy. In an article about Nicholas Roerich, an Indian journalist, R. C. Tandan, wrote: "It has been often pointed out that the paintings executed by Roerich in 1913 and in the beginning of 1914 were of prophetic nature. Some students of Roerich's art have ranged a list of titles from his works from 1897 to 1932 to show how at each step we find symbolical prophecies of coming world events."

At the opening of the 20th century, in 1901, he exhibited his three paintings *The Ravens, The Ill-Omened* and *The Ominous*, representing black ravens on dreary landscapes. The dark silhouettes of the painted ravens forbode ill for the new century. And have not the two most devastating wars in the history of mankind taken place in this 20th century?

In a biography of Nicholas Roerich, the Soviet art critic

V. P. Kniazeva comments thus on one of these sombre paintings: "It is not by chance that many have accepted the painting as a certain symbol of the epoch, as a unique prediction by the artist of inevitable calamities that awaited Russia."*

Shortly before World War I Nicholas Roerich wrote an article about his premonitions: "Soon you will know—fears and horrors will come, and then you will remember!"

S. Jay Kaufman, writing in *The Globe* (U.S.A.) thus appraised the works of Roerich: "Roerich is a seer because in 1913 and 1914 his paintings prophesied the war with its havoc and terrible aftermath."

In 1906 Nicholas Roerich created his *Battle* which shows boats with armoured warriors on a background of a cold northern sea. This picture has been interpreted as a vision of naval battles in the North Sea during the 1914-1918 War.

In 1912 the artist produced *Heaven's Battle* where golden, blue and green thunder clouds confront each other in a symbolic sky battle. How helpless look the lakes and huts below! This was a prophecy on canvas about the war clouds gathering over Europe.

The Last Angel was exhibited in the same year. An apocalyptic angel with a spear and shield hovers in cloud and smoke over a country aflame. The following lines came to Roerich as he stood before the easel: "And the beautiful, ever beautiful, the terrible, ever terrible Last Angel flew over the earth." The painting is a dramatic prediction of a world conflagration which broke out two years later.

The Cry of the Serpent, painted in 1913, presents dark-blue mountains piercing into a deep fiery-yellow sky and a ruby-coloured serpent writhing below. The theme of this work is an Eastern legend which tells of a serpent that utters a cry of warning in the face of a coming calamity. It expressed Roerich's fears for the future.

*V. P. Kniazeva, *Roerich*, Leningrad, 1963.

The Doomed City, completed early in 1914, carries a similar message. A gigantic python coils around a white city at the foot of a hill. Maxim Gorky was so impressed by it that he bought the painting. By the symbolism of this work Nicholas Roerich prophesied the doom of many a city in the Great War which began six months later.

The Messenger (1914) portrays a ship drifting towards a steep rock. The masts resemble graveyard crosses and the vessel looks like the phantom *Flying Dutchman*. Bird-like clouds, like messengers, bring ill tidings. "Awful premonitions, a feeling of painful gloom and uncertainty are felt in the painting," writes Kniazeva.

The Three Crowns, painted early in 1914, shows three kings standing with swords on a seashore. But their crowns are rising from their heads and melting into the clouds. This painting augured the end of the Hohenzollern, Hapsburg and Romanoff dynasties in the war which flared up later in the year.

The Lurid Glare, of March 1914, depicts a knight with a heavy sword on the background of a castle silhouetted on a fiery sky. Here is how Nicholas Roerich himself explained its meaning: "I completed the painting *The Lurid Glare* in March 1914. On the background of a Belgian castle by a sculpture of the Belgian lion, an armoured knight stood on guard. The whole sky was already lit by a blood-red fiery glare. But the noble knight was awake on his steady watch. Four months later it became known that this noble knight was, of course, King Albert himself, who had protected the honour of the Belgian lion."

One cannot but agree with Theodore Heline who writes that: "It is to be noted that pictorial warnings came when such upheaval as presently overtook the world was looked upon generally as virtually impossible."*

*T. Heline, *The Voice of an Epoch*, Los Angeles, 1948.

In 1916, only a year before the Russian Revolution, Roerich painted *The Three Joys*. It was a period when Russia was bleeding badly in the conflict with Germany, Austria-Hungary and Turkey. Yet the painting was devoted to Russia with an optimistic prophecy. The work shows a Russian farm with an idyllic background of hills, grazing cattle and wheatfields. Its theme is a Russian folk song about a happy peasant who is helped by the three saints—St. Elias who harvests his wheat, St. Nicholas who looks after his cows, and St. George who tends his horses. The saints are portrayed in the picture behind the farm. Here Roerich expressed his hope in the bright future of the Russian peasant. The Revolution came the following year, bringing vast improvements in the lot of the peasant, as Nicholas Roerich had predicted.

The Russian-born artist, who spent a great deal of his life in India and died there in 1947, must have had the ability to see into the future. Many of his paintings prove this supposition. A few months before Hitler's blitz invasions, Roerich produced several tempera works which suggested his foreknowledge of the coming plight of European refugees. On a country road figures of people with scant belongings are marching on the backdrop of a gloomy sky.

Looking at a prophetic painting of Roerich one can only repeat the words of Velasquez—"not a picture but truth itself."

In 1940 the artist exhibited his work *The Fires of Victory* which shows the Great Wall of China with Chinese warriors in the foreground. In 1940 most of China was occupied by the armies of Japan and no one but a seer could have prophesied victory. Yet it did come five years later and in another four the nation became a world power under the rulership of Chairman Mao.

Between two World Wars Nicholas Roerich gave

mankind the message of a New Epoch. Most of these prophecies on canvas were painted in the vast expanse of Asia, which he traversed in his expeditions as an explorer, or at his estate in Nagar, Kulu Valley, India.

Kulu lies in the Western Himalayas, south of Ladakh and west of Tibet. The author has visited the valley and he can compare its beauty to that of Switzerland. On the background of snow-capped mountain ridges, green valleys and hoary tradition the artist created his masterpieces.

They are mostly devoted to the age-old belief of Eastern peoples in the coming of a Great Teacher who will establish an era of Righteousness and Justice.

Maitreya, the future Buddha, is the subject of many works. The sacred books of Buddhism state that the manifestation of Maitreya shall come after wars.

Star of the Hero depicts a dark-blue sky with twinkling stars. A sword-like comet cuts across the heavens. Mountains loom in the distance. Around a bonfire pilgrims listen to a tale-teller who relates the ancient Indian legend about the coming Avatar on a white horse with a comet-like sword, bringing Truth and Justice.

The Kalki Avatar, to be born in Northern Shambhala, is the theme of a number of paintings as is Ghessar Khan, the hero of Mongol-Tibetan lore. Rigden-Jyapo, the Ruler of Shambhala, the Asiatic abode of gods, is featured in several works.

Sancta Protectrix—Madonnas illustrate Roerich's motto, "Peace through Culture". He had definite ideas on world problems: "There will be no peace until people learn to discriminate between mechanical civilisation and the future culture of the spirit."

This is what Roerich writes about the New Age: "A great epoch is approaching. Many things are manifesting. The cosmic fire is again approaching the earth. The stars are manifesting the new era. But many cataclysms will occur before the new era of prosperity. Again humanity will be tested to see if the spirit has progressed sufficiently."*

In the *Heart of Asia* he writes that: "The anticipation of a great Avatar near the Bridge of Worlds exists throughout broad masses. People know of the White Horse and the Fiery Comet-like Sword, and the radiant advent of the Great Rider above the skies." He alludes here to the Brahmin tradition of the Kalki Avatar.

Whilst constantly in touch with the leaders of the Western world, he was also close to the Wise Men of the East, the custodians of an arcane tradition.

It is this ancient forgotten science that revealed to him the ebb and flow of Time. His intuitive perceptions were then described with brush or pen. "Humanity is facing coming events of cosmic greatness. The time for the construction of future culture is at hand," he writes in *Beauty and Wisdom*.

Commenting on his picture of the Kalki Avatar, the Messiah of the East who will destroy the Kali Yuga, or the Black Age, Roerich quotes from the Puranas: "First will begin an unprecedented war of all nations. Afterward brother shall rise against brother. Oceans of blood shall flow. And people shall cease to understand one another. They shall forget the meaning of the word, Teacher. But just then shall the Teachers appear and in all the corners of the world shall be heard the true teaching."

The moment of the appearance of the Kalki Avatar whom Nicholas Roerich colourfully portrays in numerous works is, according to the sacred books of India, to coincide with astronomical phenomena.

The allusion to the White Horse on which the Avatar will come might be understood in terms of the Chinese-Tibetan calendar such as, for instance, the year of the *Iron*

*N. Roerich, *Himalayas–Abode of Light*, London-Bombay, 1947.

141

Horse or 1990. On the other hand, it may indicate the name or distinguishing mark of the leader.

This calendar of Asia, based on 12-year cycles symbolised by certain animals and the five elements—earth, water, fire, iron and wood—which make a grand cycle of 60 years, is a subject in itself. It is believed in the Far East that the character of events is indicated by the symbology of each year.

When the years of the Tiger or Serpent came, the Chinese expected momentous happenings. Superstition? Possibly, and yet the coincidences are worth examining.

The Year of the Fire Serpent or 1917 was the year of the Russian Revolution which changed the entire world because of the introduction of socialism. *The Year of the Earth Serpent* (1929) was the year of the depression which shook the international system of capitalism after the Wall Street crash. *The Iron Serpent* year (1941) was the year when Hitler's panzer divisions invaded the Soviet Union, and Japan attacked Pearl Harbor. *The Year of the Water Serpent* (1953) and that of the *Wood Serpent* (1965) roughly synchronised with the escalation of the wars in Korea and Vietnam. The next serpent year, 1977, which is under the fire element, should exercise a powerful influence on world affairs.

23.   COUNT LOUIS DE HAMON

AT THE CLOSE of the last century a man used the mediaeval arts of chiromancy, astrology and Cabbala with such success that he attracted the attention of royalty and celebrities of the day. He was Count Louis de Hamon, born in Ireland, whose Norman ancestry could be traced back to Rollo, the first Duke of Normandy. It was under the pseudonym of "Cheiro" that he practised the occult sciences.

In 1894 Cheiro gave a reading to Lord Kitchener warning him of a disaster at sea in the 66th year of his life. The British general was reputed to have kept the horoscope until the day of his death in 1916, aboard the *Hampshire*.

On the insistence of the King of Italy, Count de Hamon made a forecast early in 1900 which showed that King Humbert would die "within three months". In fact, the King was assassinated at Monza in July 1900.

Among Cheiro's authenticated prophecies were the Boer War (1899-1902), and the outbreak of World War I in the middle of summer of 1914 which he expected to last about four years. He also boldly predicted the eventual independence of Ireland and India in that Victorian era of colonialism. He had even anticipated the partition of India as early as 1926, some twenty years before it actually took place: "England will give India her freedom but religious warfare will rend the country from end to end until it becomes equally divided between the Mohammedans and the followers of Buddha and Brahma"*, apparently alluding to the creation of Pakistan in a future decade.

Cheiro's most dramatic predictions concern Russia. During his stay in St. Petersburg in 1904 at the time of the Russo-Japanese War, one of the Czar's ministers, Izvolsky, asked him for an astrological forecast. Count de Hamon made the following statement: "During 1914-1917 you will be called to play a rôle in connection with another Russian war, the most terrible that Russia has ever been engaged in. You will again play a very important rôle, but I do not think you will be fated to see the end of it. You, yourself, will lose everything by this coming war and will die in poverty.†

This interview was undoubtedly the outcome of a meet-

*Cheiro's World Predictions, London, 1926.
†Confessions: Memoirs of a Modern Seer, London, 1932.

ing which Count de Hamon had in his London office with Nicholas II, without recognising his royal visitor.

The Czar came to see de Hamon in order to clarify certain points in a life reading prepared for him by Cheiro on orders from King Edward VII (then Prince of Wales). Needless to say, Cheiro was totally unaware of the identity of his visitor. This horoscope read: "Whoever the man is that these numbers and birth date represent will be haunted all his life by the horrors of war and bloodshed; that he will do his utmost to prevent them, but his destiny is bound up with some of the most far-reaching and bloodiest wars in history, and that in the end, about 1917, he will lose all he loves most by sword and strife in one form or another and he himself will meet a violent death."

In 1904 Minister Izvolsky made arrangements for Count de Hamon to attend a dinner at the Czar's summer palace in Peterhof (Petrodvoretz). When Cheiro entered the Emperor's chamber, Nicholas II was reading the London *Times*. After a brief conversation conducted in English, the Czar took a sheet of paper from a locked drawer and handed it to the seer.

"Do you recognise the writing?" asked the Czar.

"Yes, your Majesty, but may I ask how that paper first came into your possession?" said the shocked count, recognizing the reading made by him in London for an anonymous friend of the Prince of Wales.

"King Edward gave it to me," replied Nicholas II. Count de Hamon wrote later that the Czar was profoundly upset by his predictions. Their awful truthfulness was subsequently proven by history.

In January 1905 Cheiro was invited to meet Gregory Rasputin who played such a fateful part in the downfall of the Russian monarchy.

"I am a greater prophet than you," boastfully said Rasputin.

On the insistence of a friend of Rasputin, the count made the following prediction: "You will wield enormous power over others but it will be a power for evil. I foresee a violent end within a palace. You will be menaced by poison, by knife, and also by bullet. Finally, I see the icy waters of the Neva closing above you."

"Rasputin can never die," shouted Rasputin with a look of burning hatred. But he was wrong—death came eleven years later in the manner foreseen by Cheiro.

In view of these exceedingly accurate predictions of historical events, it would be safe to assume that Count de Hamon was capable of breaking the Time Barrier. The key to the door to the future may lie in the unfathomed depths of the subconscious, so little explored by science.

Count Louis de Hamon left prophecies for the future but it remains to be seen how correct they are. One of his astonishing predictions concerns an archaeological discovery to be made under the Great Pyramid at Giza:

"Beneath the thirteen acre base of the pyramid a treasure temple will be discovered, one not only containing gold and jewels beyond the wildest dreams of imagination, but revealing scientific secrets by which the pyramid was built, which will upset all previously known laws relating to astronomy, gravitation, electricity, the harnessing of the powers of light, etheric rays and the hidden forces of the atom."*

The seer also believed that mankind was entering an era of sudden geological cataclysms which would spread all over the globe. He predicted that a new ridge of land will appear in the Atlantic, causing the Gulf Stream to alter its course. This could radically change the climate of the northern hemisphere, he said. De Hamon wrote of

*Cheiro's World Predictions, London, 1926.

the rising of the submerged continent of Atlantis and the resulting earthquakes, volcanic eruptions and tidal waves.

24. EDGAR CAYCE—THE AMERICAN TIME TRAVELLER

AN AMERICAN was working in his garden some seventy years ago. Looking up he saw a fiery Armada of airships, noiseless yet menacing. He ran into his house and began to pray. The man knew that a hideous war, taking millions of victims, would soon come. That is how he explained his behaviour to his family. It was not long before World War I broke out to destroy millions of soldiers in the course of that historical calamity. The man's name was Edgar Cayce who, by going into a trance, could diagnose any disease without any medical knowledge.

On numerous occasions he had pierced the veil of Time by his amazing precognitive power. When World War I was over, he made a statement duly recorded in the files of the Association for Research and Enlightenment, Inc., Virginia Beach, Virginia. This document read that "if the Versailles Conference succeeded, the world would experience a millennium. If it failed, the world would see the same elements plunging humanity into a second and far more terrible war by 1940." We now know that World War II began in September 1939 and that the world was aflame in 1940.

Cayce made other predictions of coming events, besides wars, which seemed improbable at the time. He is credited with a forecast of the Wall Street crash and the Depression, the independence of India, Hitler's downfall and the rise of the Soviet Union.

Edgar Cayce left a prophecy about a treasure buried in Giza under the Sphinx and one of the Pyramids. It contains historical records of Atlantis including a message as to who would discover the sealed vault. He described the location of the secret underground chamber "as the sun rises from the waters—as the line of the shadow (or light) falls between the paws of the Sphinx." Cayce was certain that the archives include the whole history of the vanished Atlantean civilisation.

This storehouse of records, or "time capsule", contains tablets and documents of Atlantean and early Egyptian origin. Mummies, gold and precious stones, surgical instruments and even a complete record on how the Pyramids were built by the employment of levitation, are to be found inside this crypt.

"The Sleeping Prophet" believed that a vast cataclysm would be impending between 1958 and 1998, due mainly to the shifting of the poles. He predicted eruptions of volcanoes, appearance of land in the Atlantic as well as in the Pacific. Cayce placed San Francisco and Los Angeles on the danger list. The catastrophe will be gradual but New York will be hit. The waters of the Great Lakes will empty into the Gulf of Mexico, instead of the Atlantic.

New land will rise in the Caribbean. The contours of northern Europe will be changed. There will be geological upheavals on the north and south poles as well. South America will be shaken and a portion of the bed of the Atlantic will rise. Japan, on the contrary, will sink. But Edgar Cayce promised there would be ample warning. These displacements of continents will cause great climatic changes. When Atlantis rises, archaeologists will discover a temple on the new island, containing ancient records.

He was not pessimistic about our destiny even with a half-ruined New York. Cayce expected the city to be eventually rebuilt in a future when mankind will travel in "cigar-shaped aircraft" at supersonic speeds. The time cliché of the future he saw was dated about the year 2100.

Violent earthquakes and floods were foretold by Edgar

Cayce but he said nothing about building a 20th-century ark. In fact he believed in the Coming Millennium and thought that the peace of the world would be shaped upon the Masonic ideal of Brotherhood. He promised that towards the end of this century mankind would have spiritual understanding.

25.   JEANE DIXON—THE SIBYL OF WASHINGTON

"THERE ARE many fortune-tellers but few true prophets," said the Oracle of Delphi. This is as true of the modern world as it was of ancient Greece, for the gift of prophecy is as rare as a pearl at the bottom of the sea. The distinctive marks of a genuine prediction are its improbability and the accuracy with which it is described. The prophecies of Jeane Dixon, of Washington, D.C., certainly possess both characteristics.

Jeane Dixon does not commercialise on her amazing ability to predict future events. With her husband, James Dixon, she conducts a successful real estate agency in Washington. Generally, Mrs. Dixon is known as the "Seeress of the Capitol."

Late in 1944, while World War II was still raging in Europe and Asia, President Franklin D. Roosevelt summoned her to the White House. He wanted to know how much time he had to complete his mission. Mrs. Dixon replied that in view of his failing health the President did not have more than six months.

In answer to President Roosevelt's question, Jeane Dixon said that the relations with Russia would deteriorate until about a generation later when the United States and the Union of Soviet Socialist Republics would form an alliance against "Red China". In 1944 China was under Japanese occupation except for a few provinces ruled from Chungking by Chiang Kai-shek. Mao Tse-tung was then chief of the Red partisans. Roosevelt was astonished to hear about "Red China" as much as anyone would have been at the time. Red China and Africa would be the greatest problems of the future, said Mrs. Dixon.

Two years before the partition of India, Jeane Dixon made a prophecy to that effect. At a reception in Washington in 1945 she told sceptical Colonel Nawabjaba Sher Ali, the Military Attaché, that India would be divided on June 2, 1947. When the separation of India and Pakistan occurred on that date, Earl Jellicoe, the U.K. Embassy Secretary in the U.S.A., wanted to clarify a question. Two days ago, he said, the House of Commons had rejected the partition. How could Mrs. Dixon foresee not only two days but two years in advance what would happen in India? "I saw it in the crystal ball," answered Jeane Dixon to the baffled diplomat.

Winston Churchill attended a party given in his honour by Lord and Lady Halifax in the capital of the United States in early 1945. Mrs. Dixon, who was present, advised him to delay election because of the possibility of a defeat. "England will never let me down," grumbled the wartime leader of Great Britain. But in July of that year Winston Churchill was defeated and replaced by Prime Minister Attlee.

In Chaing Kai-shek's Embassy in Washington, Jeane Dixon made a startling prophecy in October 1946. "China will go Communist," she predicted. True enough, the Red Flag waved over all of China three years later.

The Seeress of Washington anticipated the plane accident in Africa in which the United Nations Secretary General Dag Hammarskjold lost his life.

In the middle of 1947 Jeane Dixon announced that Mahatma Gandhi would be killed within six months. The great leader of India was assassinated on January 30, 1948.

Parade magazine published a feature story on Jeane Dixon in the May 13, 1956, issue which said that the 1960 election would be won by a Democrat who might be assassinated. She described this future President, as early as 1952 and then in 1956, as a young, tall and blue-eyed man with thick brown hair. The resemblance of this portrait to John F. Kennedy became obvious after his election as President of the United States in 1960.

Three months before John Kennedy's assassination in November 1963, Jeane Dixon went to see Kay Halle, a friend of the Kennedys. Mrs. Dixon apologised for the unexpected visit and explained that, since Kay Halle knew the President personally, an important message had to reach him. He was not to go to the South, and must cancel the trip as it might be fatal to him. Miss Halle refused to give the warning to a man of such courage as John Kennedy. This raises the ever-recurrent philosophical question in connection with freewill. Had the warning been given, would Kennedy have changed his plans? Probably his character would not have allowed him to heed it. It is a known fact that John Kennedy ordered the plexiglass safety bubble to be removed from his car.

Jeane Dixon thought it was her moral duty to bring the danger menacing the President to the attention of the Federal Bureau of Investigation. Three days before the assassination, she carried out this plan. But the F.B.I. and Central Intelligence Agency work on facts and not on premonitions. The security officers ignored the warning and John Kennedy was killed.

One of the most spectacular prophecies ever made by Mrs. Dixon concerns the launching of Sputnik I. On an N.B.C. television programme, broadcast from Washington, D.C., she forecast on May 14, 1953, that a silver ball would come from Russia to spin in space. In the course of the television programme, Jeane Dixon held out her hands to indicate the size of the satellite. At a period when space travel was solidly in the realm of science fiction, not many people in America took her seriously. But the Soviet Ambassador in the United States—George Zarubin—sent her an invitation for an interview with him.

"Where did you learn such information about a Russian space programme?" the bewildered diplomat asked. The answers Jeane Dixon gave did not impress the U.S.S.R. Ambassador as much as the actual launching of Sputnik I in 1957.

Appearing on the same television programme with *Mission to Moscow* Davies, a former U.S. Ambassador to Moscow, she predicted the fall of Malenkov in less than two years. He would be replaced by a man with an oval-shaped head, wavy grey hair, a little goatee and greenish eyes. The response from Davies was jeers. But in 1955 goateed Marshal Bulganin took over from Malenkov exactly as the Seeress of the Capitol predicted in 1953. Then she said that the next man in the Kremlin would be a short bald-headed man who would contribute to world peace. It was during his administration that the "silver ball" was to zoom in space. His power would last only a few years, Mrs. Dixon said. In the portrait we now recognise Khrushchev.

Many years ago the Seeress of Washington predicted a Republican victory in the 1968 elections.

"Our dollar position will become precarious," wrote Mrs. Dixon in 1969, also hinting at the possible rise in the price of gold. Both forecasts were fulfilled in 1972-1973.

Jeane Dixon does not claim to be infallible as she does not believe in absolute predestination. On certain occasions she has been able to forestall accidents. Her husband, James L. Dixon, was wise enough to heed one of her warnings when she asked him to cancel an air trip. The plane on which he held a ticket crashed near Chicago, leaving no survivors.

Jeane Dixon has made significant predictions in regard to the next thirty years. The colour problem in the U.S.A. will not be solved before 1980. There will be incidents on the U.S.S.R.–China border. She expects a great war with Red China in the eighties, with the United States and Russia allied in the conflict. Parts of Africa and the Far East will be on the side of China. The Chinese may employ "germ warfare" against the Soviet Union and America in that world conflagration.

There is a danger of a Pope being harmed, says Mrs. Dixon. The throne of St. Peter will become empty but the light of Christianity will remain. About the time of this terrible war with China a great spiritual leader will arise to lay the foundation of an era of peace. He was born on February 5, 1962, at a time of the rare conjunction of seven planets, the first of its kind in four hundred years. On that day there was great commotion in India because of a prediction of an imminent end to our epoch.

Mrs. Dixon believes that this child with "all-knowing eyes" was born in the Middle East to a poor peasant family, and is a descendant of Queen Nefertiti and Pharaoh Amenhotep, who established the cult of One God centuries before Biblical monotheism. The great reformer will combine all religions and ideologies into one doctrine which will revolutionise the world. War and the suffering associated with it will end once and for all. The revolutionary leader will spread his teaching from the early eighties and by 1999 his power will reach all the peoples on earth.

In her book* Jeane Dixon shows her apprehension, even bias, about this coming avatar, on the ground that his mission would be "anti-Christian" and "pagan" in character. This is semantics, for what is Christianity—the

*J. Dixon, *My Life and Prophecies*, London, 1969.

established churches with their record of the Thirty Years War and the present sectarian bloodshed in Ulster? Or is it a simple doctrine of peace and non-violence? And it should not be overlooked that there are more non-Christians on this planet than Christians.

In one of her visions Jeane Dixon saw a comet striking the earth and causing untold upheavals and loss of life in the middle 1980s. This astronomical body will hit one of the oceans, claims Jeane Dixon.

26. FROM BULLFIGHTING TO THE CONQUEST OF TIME

IN ROSSVILLE, Georgia, resides Robert Charles Anderson, known as "Doc" Anderson because of his miraculous cures. He first became aware of his faculty of clairvoyance at the age of nine when a mental vision of his brother being killed in an accident suddenly flashed before him.

Inspired by the romantic tales of his Spanish mother, Robert Anderson became a bullfighter, gaining recognition as Roman style world champion in the years 1930-1935.

Then he decided to take Time by the horns instead of the bull and began to study Time clichés of people's lives with a view to helping them to solve problems. Occasionally, he has received impressions of the shape of things to come and told his friends about them.

On Christmas Day, 1944, R. C. Anderson issued a signed statement, witnessed by three persons and a Notary Public, a photostatic copy of which is in my possession.

"I predict that—owing to the poor health and the great demands made upon him—President Roosevelt will not live his term out, and that he will pass away about the middle of April, 1945," reads one paragraph of this document. When the radio announced the President's death, the local police chief with two government agents arrived at "Doc's" office and took him for questioning.

"I predict that we will create a devastating device, that will tear the elements apart in its intensity, and that something will happen about the earlier part of August 1945, which will change the whole course of the war against Japan, and I further predict that the war with Japan will come to an end about ten days later." This is an accurate prophecy of the explosion of the atom-bomb over Hiroshima, and the subsequent capitulation of Japan.

"I predict that, with the development and use of the principles of the adiabatic expansion of air, aeroplanes will travel faster than sound and propulsion will reach unbelievable results," reads another forecast, written in the pre-jet age.

"I predict that, through the medium of rocket propulsion, various attempts will be made to place a man-made planet into the stratosphere. I predict that the early attempts to do so will be met with total failure and that success in this direction will not be accomplished until about 1958 or 1959. I predict that by 1968 inteplanetary travel will become an accomplished fact, and that we will have a manned station on the moon," claimed Anderson in 1944, a quarter of a century before the Apollo missions to the moon.

In the same document he pointed to the great unrest which would spread throughout the Middle East, Africa, India and the Far East. This prophecy has been fulfilled with the collapse of the colonialist system.

In a letter addressed to the author and dated March 18, 1968, "Doc" Anderson wrote about coming violence in Czechoslovakia, caused by an attempt to subdue the bid for liberalisation. This came true six months later.

But the clairvoyant is not infallible. "Anderson predicts

154

Wallace will be President of United States," said the headlines of a southern newspaper a few years ago. Although Governor Wallace won more votes than expected in the last Presidential election in America, he was never nominated Presidential candidate by the Democrats. In fact, an attempt on his life was made at the time. It may well be that political or religious feelings can cloud the vision of a seer.

Now what does Anderson prophesy for the future? The next great war will come from China but it will be short-lived. In this conflict the United States and the Soviet Union will ally against China. This is what "Doc" Anderson predicted in 1968. Fortunately, he made no mention of the use of nuclear weapons in this future war.

However, before the end of the century, war as we know it today will be completely abolished and the whole world will be one.

R. C. Anderson prophesies geological cataclysms for the latter part of the 20th century: "The world will experience violent earthquakes in sections of the world never detected before. There will be a change in the Gulf Stream resulting in radical weather changes."

The seer of Dixieland has described the inhabitants of Venus who, he thinks, would be discovered on that planet. "Life will be found on Venus in the form of human life, almost in the form we know. The pigment of their skin is different, and there is a marked difference in the location and use of their eyes. Their form of communication is also different from ours," he said in 1968. This prediction will naturally be met with scepticism and ridicule by astronomers who do not expect to find any life on that intensely hot planet.

"To those who dream in a waking state are revealed many things which evade those who dream only at night," wrote Edgar Allan Poe in *Eleanora.* Perhaps Anderson may be one of these exceptional dreamers.

27. THE DECISIVE DECADES

BY USING imagination and logic we can create a minia-ture model of the Big World of Tomorrow. Manifold problems loom in the future, and it is not clear how they can be solved.

At the time of Napoleon Bonaparte 1,000 million people dwelt on Earth. There will be 7,000 million Earthmen in the year 2000, mostly concentrated in already over-populated Asia. Unless population control, resettlement, food production and distribution are operated on a global scale, starvation faces many a country in the immediate future.

Every young man and woman born after 1945 has radio-strontium in his or her bones. They are the true children of the Atomic Age. Will more radioactivity be added to our atmosphere? Our air is also polluted by the smoke from chimneys, incinerators and car carburettors. Water supplied to our giant cities often contains detergents and chlorine. Noise pollution from automobiles, motor-cycles, trucks and jets has an unfavourable effect on the nervous system and is producing a generation of neuras-thenics.

Futurology, the new art of scientific prediction, is becoming more and more important in our complex world. *The Year 2000*, termed by the authors, Herman Kahn and Anthony J. Wiener, as "a framework of specu-lation on the next thirty three years," contains "scenarios" of the future based on present-day political, economic, scientific and ideological trends.

Questions of world order and stability are analysed in these "scenarios" of tomorrow's history. They are not predictions but imaginative and authenticated pictures of what *might happen* between now and the year 2000.

While forecasting the progress of science and technology, the work warns about nuclear and other "nightmares", and defends the humanist position of man as architect of his own destiny.

These two American "think-tank" scientists write that "by the year 2000 computers are likely to match, simulate or surpass some of man's most 'human-like' intellectual abilities."

The life-story of a citizen will be recorded in a central computer bank. Parents will select the sex and personal characteristics of their children through genetic control.

Space platforms, lunar and planetary installations will be constructed before the end of the century. Undersea colonies will be built on the bottom of the oceans.

Computers in industry and at home will become common, and new sources of power may be discovered, state Kahn and Wiener in their authoritative book.

All this is valid, of course, only if in the meantime we do not get poisoned from polluted air, water or food or, still worse, become extinct as a result of a global nuclear war. The choice is ours.

But there are things which man cannot control such as natural resources. Total oil reserves of our planet are sufficient only for the next thirty years. After that the internal combustion engines, that is motor cars, will be displayed only in museums.

Uranium, zinc, mercury, tin and lead will be exhausted by 1990-1995. There is enough copper to last until 2010 and nickel until 2030. Our technology is facing difficult problems in the years ahead.

Science has played the rôle of a soothsayer. It can predict its own advances in astronautics and medicine.

Astronomy is in a position to pinpoint the date of the appearance of a comet. Demology can accurately estimate the growth of the world's population. All these conclusions are drawn from the theory of probability.

The most conservative and unimaginative scientist of today realises that on the dark background of deadly nuclear weapons, the monster of nationalism, fast-growing global population and equally fast-dropping food resources, the seventies, eighties and the nineties will be the most decisive decades in world history. To these problems should be added the introduction of automation, regulation of economics, and the preservation of co-existence with the socialist world.

It was Einstein who said that if World War III is fought with atomic bombs, the armies in World War IV will use clubs.

Most of the pressing problems can be resolved if solutions are sought on a planetary level before the end of this critical century.

Valuable as the forecasts of the future from scientific sources are, they allow only a narrow margin for the improbable. On the surface of the sea of history it is the unforeseen gales that rule. To predict the impossible may be a task for the prophets.

On the path to the future one must be ready for new landscapes and faces. Our inability to foresee tomorrow is the result of sitting on the Time Barrier.

The prognostications offered in this book for the critical attention of the reader may or may not be correct. But there is nothing supernatural about these predictions. A giant computer, properly programmed in order to process up-to-the-minute data from all fields of human activity, could also prophesy. In fact, oil companies use electronic brains to determine the quantity of oil to be refined on the basis of past petrol consumption, weather forecasts and other factors. So do the T.V. stations in ascertaining the popularity value of future programmes

Do the seers use their minds like computers? This is an open question because so little is known about the mind. As Professor J. B. Rhine once remarked: "We know the atom far better than we know the mind that knows the atom."

It is not an idle occupation to try to glimpse down the road which men will take in the immediate future.

A strange fact becomes evident in studying the forecasts presented in this book—they have many points in common. They all predict disasters for the end of this century to be followed by a Golden Age. To cite from Milton's *Paradise Lost*—

The world shall burn, and from her ashes spring
New heaven and earth, wherein the just shall dwell . . .

It is apparent that the predictions of the seers of former centuries and present times have an infinitely small element of probability in them.

The more sceptical readers may altogether discard the foreknowledge of the future as talk of "dreams, which are the children of an idle brain, begot of nothing but vain fantasy," as Shakespeare put it.

Rather than listen to the raving prophets they may prefer to get ready for the Golden Age of Science which is already at our doorstep. In that marvellous age we shall live in one-hundred-storeyed reinforced concrete towers, eat only chemically produced foods, dress in synthetics, use pushbuttons for housework and entertainment.

At least science and the prophets agree on one score— the Golden Age is in the Book of Time though the road to it may be bumpy.

For his destiny the reader has the privilege to choose the Paradise of Automation, the Cosmic Millennium of the seers, or his own new order.

159

CONCLUSION

The progress of science is nothing more than a constant quest for new explanations to the old facts of Nature.

This book does not contain ultimate answers to the enigma of Time but opens new avenues leading to its solution.

The Theory of Relativity states that the Time rate is dependent on atomic processes. In the fabulously fast flight of a photon space rocket, its fuselage and everything within would undergo a slowing-down of all atomic oscillation. A retardation of Time would then follow and long centuries would seem like a few brief years to the astronauts in interstellar space. Theoretically, an artificial acceleration of atomic processes can result in a corresponding speeding-up of Time, and a year would be lived in hours.

Not only the rate of Time but even its direction can be changed in the nuclear world. The Time arrow is caused by asymmetry of negative and positive electric charges in the atomic world. What is the future to us may be already the past to a mankind in the antiworld.

An imaginary cosmic chronicler may have been registering events every minisecond since the creation of our galaxy. But in the antiworld another recorder may have been keeping a similar book since the end of our world! The two chronicles, bound together, would form the Book of Time in which past and future exist side by side. It appears that seers are able to read in that Book.

The puzzling phenomenon of Time reverberations, or apparitions of the past, deserves the attention of science. It may reveal how yesterday could be brought back to life and shown on the screen of the Time Television set.

To pull down the Time Barrier and see the future or the past is an achievement as great as launching a space probe.

The true conclusion to this book will really be written in Time by Time itself.